A **MAN** AND HIS **STORY**

A **MAN** AND HIS **STORY**

Published by Authentic Manhood
Copyright 2012 Fellowship Associates Inc.
First Printing 2012

ISBN: 978-1-4158-7552-0
Item: 005537107

Project Management & Art Direction: Brian Jones
Design: Mike Robinson, Details Communications
Editors: Rick Caldwell, Grant Edwards, Brian Jones, Rachel Lindholm, Amanda Magdefrau, Steve Snider, Rebekah Wallace, Lindsey Woodward
Contributors: Hunter Beaumont, John Bryson, Bryan Carter, Chip Dodd, Grant Edwards, Brian Goins, Tierce Green, Grant Guffin, Brian Jones, Cliff Jordan, Jeff D. Lawrence, Eric Mason, James Pecht, Will Stacy

Authentic Manhood, Men's Fraternity and 33 The Series are registered trademarks of Fellowship Associates Inc.

To order additional copies of this resource, go to **authenticmanhood.com** or contact Lifeway Church Resources online at **lifeway.com** or visit a Lifeway Christian Store nearest you.

Printed in the United States of America

Distributed by:

Authentic Manhood
12115 Hinson Rd, Suite 200
Little Rock, AR 72113

Leadership and Adult Publishing
LifeWay Church Resources
One LifeWay Plaza
Nashville, TN 37234-0175

TABLE of CONTENTS

How to Experience 33 as an Individual or Group

33 The Series can be viewed on DVD, downloaded from **authenticmanhood.com**, or experienced via mobile apps. Any of these three delivery systems can be utilized by groups or individuals. *One of the great things about this series is the variety of ways it can be used and/or presented.*

The series is organized in a way that provides flexibility and offers a variety of options on how the material can be experienced. *33* is organized into six topically-themed volumes that include six sessions each. *Volumes include topics on a man's design, story, traps, parenting, marriage and career.* You can choose to commit to one volume/topic at a time, by limiting a particular experience to six sessions, or you can combine multiple volumes into one expanded experience that includes more sessions (12, 18, 24, 30, or 36). You can also choose any combination thereof.

However you choose to experience 33, the manhood principles and practical insights taught in each volume are essential for every man on the journey to Authentic Manhood. 33

The Importance of Being in a **Community of Men**

Climbing a mountain alone is a difficult and even dangerous undertaking. Attempting to climb the mountain of manhood alone is also not recommended. Just like a mountain climber needs to belay or connect with another man for safety and support, we need other men around us to help us stay on course with our manhood.

Having other men deeply connected to us becomes invaluable when we slip, struggle, or stray off course in our manhood journey.

To fully enjoy 33, experience it in community with other men. The goal of this study is not just to fill in the blanks of your **Training Guide,** but also to fill in the blanks of your life. Having other men walk through the experience with you is key to moving this material from the pages of your **Training Guide** to the pages of your life.

MANHOOD COMMUNITY

1 Provides encouragement. Every man needs other men cheering for him and encouraging him on his journey to Authentic Manhood.

2 Gives you additional insight. Having other men around you helps you get a much better perspective on your life. Others can help you discover your blind spots and avoid costly mistakes.

3 Brings constructive criticism. We all need men in our lives who will be honest with us to help us become better men.

4 Makes your journey richer. Sharing life with a community of men makes the great times feel like a celebration and provides much needed support when life gets rough.

No one can force you to open up your life and work to make a connection with another man. Although it can be challenging and frightening, it's well worth the risk. **33**

From a **Weekly Gathering** to a **Global Movement**

Several years ago, Dr. Robert Lewis responded to the desire of a handful of men who were hungering for more than a Bible study. They wanted a map for manhood – a definition of what it meant to be a man. They needed help to leap over the hurdles they were encountering in life.

Robert responded by launching a weekly gathering called Men's Fraternity, challenging men to join him at six o'clock each Wednesday morning for 24-weeks. From the depth of his own personal experience and the pages of Scripture, Robert developed what came to be known as the Men's Fraternity series:

• *The Quest for Authentic Manhood*
• *Winning at Work & Home*
• *The Great Adventure*

What began with a few men huddling up grew into a weekly gathering of more than 300 men. In just a few years, local attendance at Men's Fraternity climbed to more than a thousand men.

The message of Authentic Manhood began to spread and soon exploded into a global movement *impacting more than a million men in more than 20,000 locations worldwide* – from locker rooms to boardrooms, from

churches to prisons, on military bases and the field of battle, at NASA and even on a space shuttle mission. Wherever the messages were heard, the challenge remained the same: to call men to step up and follow biblical manhood modeled by Jesus Christ.

The Men's Fraternity curriculum *was created on the front lines where men live, written in the trenches in response to men who pleaded for purpose and direction.* It has proven to be the most widely used and effective material on Authentic Manhood available today.

What began as a weekly meeting of men searching for answers to their manhood questions has grown into a bold movement that has dramatically impacted the lives of men, their families and communities. 33

A Movement that Grows Authentic Men and Plants Churches

For over a decade, Fellowship Associates has helped over *a million men all over the world to discover the life of truth, passion and purpose they were created to live through Authentic Manhood materials.* During that same decade, Fellowship Associates has been directing a church planting residency program that has been recognized as one of the most effective church planting efforts in the world.

The proceeds from the sale of Authentic Manhood materials have helped underwrite the planting of 56 (and growing) strategic churches throughout the United States as well as in Canada, Hong Kong, Dubai, Guatemala, Poland, and Spain. 33

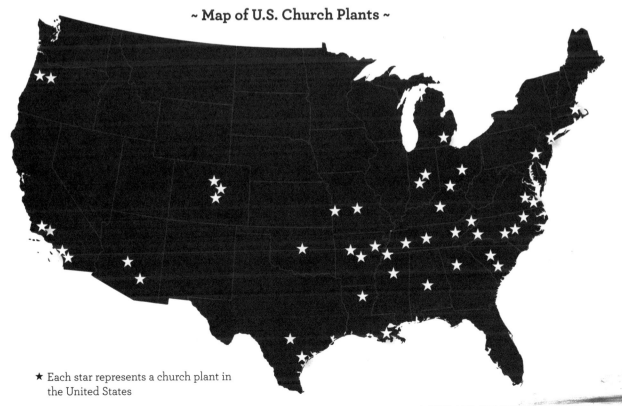

~ Map of U.S. Church Plants ~

★ Each star represents a church plant in the United States

33
THE SERIES™

The **Presenters**

BRYAN CARTER

Bryan Carter taught the original Men's Fraternity curriculum to a group of more than 800 men over a three-year period at Concord Church. Additionally, he's been a frequent speaker at local and international churches, conferences and events.

Bryan is the Senior Pastor of Concord Church in Dallas, Texas.

He is the author of a 28-day devotional book entitled, *Great Expectations*. Bryan also contributed to the book *What Two White Men of God Learned from Black Men of God,* coauthored by Dr. Joel Gregory and Dr. Bill Crouch.

A recreational basketball player, Bryan is a fan of the NBA's Dallas Mavericks.

Bryan and his wife Stephanie are the parents of two daughters, Kaitlyn and Kennedy, and one son, Carson.

TIERCE GREEN

Tierce Green teaches the principles of Authentic Manhood to well over a thousand men each week at a gathering called *The Quest*. He is also one of the teaching pastors in the bullpen for his Senior Pastor, Kerry Shook.

Tierce is the Executive Pastor of Small Groups at Woodlands Church in The Woodlands, Texas.

Tierce has written curriculum for Student Life, North American Mission Board and LifeWay. His most recent project is a 12-week series for men called *Fight Club: Some Things Are Worth Fighting For*.

A lifelong Dallas Cowboys fan, Tierce's favorite activities include landscaping, good food and conversation.

He and his wife Dana have one daughter, Anna.

JOHN BRYSON

Seeing firsthand the impact the original Men's Fraternity curriculum had on his own life, John Bryson decided to teach the material himself. In the years since, he's led thousands of men through the basic ideas of biblical manhood.

John is a co-founding teaching pastor of Fellowship Memphis in Memphis, Tennessee.

In 2010, he completed his Doctor of Ministry from Gordon-Conwell Theological Seminary. John is also the author of *College Ready,* a curriculum for college students, and travels the country consulting and investing in churches, church planters, leaders and new ideas.

A native of Harlan, Kentucky, John played baseball at Asbury College.

He and his wife Beth have 5 kids: Brooke, Beck, Bo, Boss and Blair.

Looking Back

SESSION **ONE** | Training Guide

THIS SERIES CAN ALSO BE EXPERIENCED IN THE 33 APP

★Home Run

by Chip Dodd

My name is Chip Dodd.

I have worked in the world of restoration of men's hearts for over 25 years. I have a PhD and am a licensed professional. The words you are about to read I mean, and I live.

The life we are meant to have is not just about intellect, willpower or morality as much as it is about giving our hearts to the God who loves us and to the people who need us. In so doing, we ourselves can be blessed to live fully, love deeply and lead well.

We cannot give what we do not know and do

evening was calm. The day was finished. Life was good. From the backseat my youngest son William said, "Dad, do you remember when I hit the home run at McKnight Field?" I heard him clearly, but wanted to say, "What?" as if I misunderstood so that maybe he would say, "Never mind" or "Nothing." You see, I knew that he had not actually hit a home run but a ball that bounced over the fence. He wished deeply that the hit could be a home run and was seeking my affirmation of his "success."

His brother, Tennyson, had already hit a passel of home runs that summer and had stowed the balls away in a drawer in his bedroom, with the

Heartbreak

not have. **We have to be able to know the heart and use the language of the heart to be able to give heart and fully understand our story.** God wants to give us an abundant life, yet we have to show up to receive it with our hearts in our hands.

What follows below is an abridged story from my book, *The Perfect Loss.* I wrote the book as a testimony of what God can do with a surrendered heart.

■■ When my youngest son, William, was eight years old and oldest son Tennyson was ten, my wife and I and the boys were driving home one Friday night after going out to eat. The

trophies from the team's championships. He also had a nickname, T-Bone, which became memorable to other boys and interested parents.

I said to William truthfully and gently, "No." Then, he tried again, with a little more urgency in his voice, "Yeah, Dad, you remember. I hit the ball and it bounced over the fence and everybody thought it was a home run, but really it bounced over, but it was a home run. You remember."

I felt more fear and a dawning pain of compassion pulling at my heart. I slowly said, "No, William, I don't remember that."

After hearing me say, "No," William sat for a second; then he screamed from the backseat, "Don't say that! Don't say that! Yes, I did; you remember!" The silence in the car was heavy and a thousand words of heart sat on a tipping point, to either be brought into the light or to fall into the dark of unsettled shadows and squashed dreams. My little eight-year old son beckoned me to meet him in his expression of pain while he was telling me to leave him alone.

The part of me that just didn't want to deal with this and didn't know what to do wanted to run

I love you for you.

★
★
★
★

away from William's pain—ignore him or "teach him about life." **I just wanted to fix it by telling him something that I didn't know to be true: "You will hit a home run next time." I wanted to postpone his agony by pretending a gushing cut was just a scratch.** I wanted to attack what I could not control, shut him down with my own denial about life's outcomes and tell him to toughen up. I wanted to give him a resignation pill—the infamous fix-all—"Life's not fair, so get over it and get on with it." This half-truth always works to shame hope into a corner. I said none of these things.

We drove home in silence. I hurt inside about my young son. I knew pain. I knew what it was like to hide my heart, to pour contempt upon hope, to mock the risk of vulnerability, and to lose dreams without grieving. My William was in pain. I knew he needed someone to fight for him so he could have himself back and his destiny—to show up emotionally and spiritually.

We arrived home while I was having these thoughts. As we got out of the vehicle and headed toward the back door, I said, "William, stay out here with me; let's sit out here." He said, "No, sir." I sat down where I believe God had designed for us to sit, on our back porch, looking out over our courtyard of flowers and bushes on an old church pew.

William said, "No" again, then sat down, the way someone sits when they are still standing up on the inside. We sat there. He, staring out into the dark, full of pain, silent. I, full of pain, scared, wanting and locked out. I reached out my hand to touch the back of his shoulder. He

pulled away with a message of contempt. I sat there seeing the back of him.

Then, I said the simplest, most obvious hopeful prayer I could imagine. "William, do you believe that you have to hit home runs to be somebody?"

Before I knew it, an anguished cry rose from within my eight-year old. "What do you think?" he cried and then the tears rushed forward as his torso fell over onto his thighs, and his head rested against his clenched hands. "What do you think? All I ever hear is 'T-Bone, T-Bone, T-Bone.' I'm nobody. They don't even know my name," he wailed. A groan emerged with chest-wracking tears as his rib cage shook. "I'll never be anybody 'til I can hit a home run." I was leaning forward with him. His tears dropped like rain on the old red bricks, turning each spot black.

I slowly reached out my hand and touched his shoulder; this time his body melted against my leg as I leaned over him with a heavy heart. After a time of crying hard, he breathed the breath that is the rest of the grieving; I said, "William, William, I don't care whether you ever hit a home run or even play baseball. You are William. Your worth is yours, your gifts are yours; you are your own kind of ball player. You will hit a home run when it's time, or your gifts will play themselves out in many other ways. I love you for you. You have got to be William. I know you want to hit home runs. I know you hurt. But you are made to be William."

Resting against my leg with the side of his face turned onto my knee, he looked tired, and rested, and like William. Some of the words I spoke went into the openings of his heart. Most of them probably just disappeared, but the love wasn't lost, nor his struggle for truthfulness wasted.

We talked quietly a little more. He said after a bit that he was ready to go inside. I asked if he minded if I prayed. Afterwards, as we entered the house off the porch, Sonya and Tennyson were coming into the same room. William saw Tennyson, moved to him quickly, put his

arms around him and said from way inside himself, "I love you, Tennyson." There they stood, arms around each other; the one who walked in pain proclaiming love to the one who, at the time, walked in victory. "I love you, too, William," were Tennyson's simple words. William had his heart back and his voice with it. I wish that none of it had to happen, but even more I was thankful that I had the heart to step into my love. **⎘⎘**

One of the longest journeys a man can take is eighteen inches, from his head to his heart. He moves from figuring to feeling so he can become all of himself. By becoming able to identify, explore and express what he is feeling, a man becomes more accessible to himself, others and God.

As men, we must bring our hearts to the surface in order to discover and tell the stories of our lives. What were we scared of back there? What hurt and maybe even still hurts? Who taught me about loving a woman? Who showed me how to be vulnerable with men? When did I become ashamed of asking questions? How did I get rage and healthy anger confused? When did survival take the place of dreams and "getting by" take the place of passion? What makes me apologize for being sad or even cry about loss? The answers to these questions are a part of my own unique story and will open up doors of shared experiences with other men who also have their own unique stories. The truth of our lives allows us to find kinship. When one man tells the truth about himself, ironically he is often telling the truth about the lives of many other men.

We are made to live fully, love deeply and lead well. We are made to do so by living a life of passion, intimacy and integrity. We find the doorway to living this life by learning how to feel our feelings, tell the truth about them and give these experiences to God and others. To find our feelings, we must identify, explore and express what is happening within us.

To live the lives we are made for and the lives that our wives, children, friends and those we lead need us to live, we have to practice a daily experience of confession, surrender and acceptance. Confession is the daily admission of being human to God. I am not God, and I am in need of God. Surrender is the giving over of our hearts to the God who made us and wants us back—everyday. Acceptance is the work of facing the fact that life is tragic but God is faithful in the midst of the tragedy. As we practice confession, surrender and acceptance, we keep an undivided heart. We also end up living a story that carries on in the hearts of those we have loved–even beyond our earthly lives.

May God bless the next phase of your story. Thank you for striving for Authentic Manhood for both yourself and for those who matter most to you. You are a gift and you live in a world that desperately needs you to show up and look back so you can give your heart. **33**

33 Presenter Insight

The **Power** of **Story**

by John Bryson, 33 Presenter

Every man has a story and every man is in the midst of a story. God is the ultimate author of all things, including my story and your story (see Romans 8:28; 11:36). A man cannot truly step into Authentic Manhood until he begins to see his life as a narrative–an epic adventure, a tragedy and a comedy all rolled up into one, with an ending that has yet to unfold!

I remember, in my twenties, being in a small group of men and being challenged by them to write down my heritage, my high points, my hurts and my heroes for the purpose of sharing my life story with the group. Being encouraged to look back, put my story on paper and share those discoveries with other men was powerful. Giving focused attention to my past, giving voice to the shaping influences of my life and sharing the good, the bad and the ugly of all that is me with trustworthy men was profound. Equally as powerful was hearing them do the same and realizing that though my story is unique, as a man, I am not alone. *We all have been shaped by defining moments, decisions, painful experiences and personal relationships.*

In my thirties, that "look back" got enhanced and nuanced as I listened to Dr. Robert Lewis teach

Men's Fraternity and the Quest for Authentic Manhood in Little Rock, Arkansas. Men's Fraternity was the movement that birthed and inspired 33 The Series. I was struck by Robert's clarity in telling his own story. His discoveries from his past were like keys that unlocked significant doors in his present. I learned from Robert that we are all deeply influenced by our fathers, mothers, friends, mentors and even our own heart.

In my forties, the role of "story" went nuclear as I invested in several significant experiences with intensive counseling. *Trusted, skilled, and trained men led me through experiences that forced me to look back into my story and explain me, to me. They helped me not only process my life experiences, but also capture the emotions that went with those experiences.* What started on those couches was a rediscovery of my heart. As a young man, I learned to live out of my head, not out of my heart. I learned to think and accomplish, but I forgot how to feel. Here's the problem: living out of your head and with your hands usually works well in school, work, and with machinery but not so well with God, your spouses, kids, and friends. Those closest to you want your heart.

It is my deep desire that every man who experiences 33 *The Series* will not only be equipped, but will also have the courage to "look back," so that he knows his story, understands his own heart, and is able to give his heart to those he loves. Chip Dodd cast a vision for me to "Live fully, love deeply and lead well;" and that is my desire for every man on the journey to Authentic Manhood. 33

Join the conversation about this article

facebook facebook.com/33theseries
twitter @33theseries

Moving Beyond the Past

by Jeff Lawrence

Jesus hand-picked Peter as a future leader of His movement. He had enormous plans for Peter, but Jesus also knew that Peter had blown it. Big time. In front of everyone. Just before Jesus had gone to His death through crucifixion, He warned Peter that he would deny Him three times. Peter said, "No way," but it happened exactly as Jesus predicted.

After Jesus' death and resurrection, He recognized that Peter would have to deal with his past before he could move forward and be the leader he was called to be. Jesus initiated a special meeting with Peter over a meal which they shared near the fishing boat–a place where Peter was comfortable. After some initial chit-chat, Jesus got to the point:

Jesus said to Simon Peter, "Simon son of John, do you love me more than these?"

"Yes, Lord," he said, "you know that I love you."

Jesus said, "Feed my lambs."

Again Jesus said, "Simon son of John, do you love me?"

He answered, "Yes, Lord, you know that I love you."

Jesus said, "Take care of my sheep."

The third time he said to him, "Simon son of John, do you love me?"

Peter was hurt because Jesus asked him the third time, "Do you love me?"

> ## "Peter needed to revisit his past in order to fully understand his story and prepare for his future."

He said, *"Lord, you know all things; you know that I love you."*

Jesus said, *"Feed my sheep."*

John 21:15-17 (NIV)

What was Jesus doing? Peter answered the question clearly the first time, yet Jesus asked it again and again. Jesus wasn't being cruel. Peter needed to revisit his past in order to fully understand his story and prepare for his future. Jesus asked three questions, one for each of Peter's denials.

I love how honest the Bible is about the struggle: Peter was hurt. Fact is, sometimes the only path to growth is through sorrow. If Peter didn't deal with the sin of his denying Jesus, he would never speak boldly for Jesus. Without this conversation, Peter certainly would carry guilt and self-doubt around in the days that followed, and, perhaps, others would have questioned Peter's trustworthiness. Peter needed restoration so that he could advance in confidence and freedom as the new leader of the church. He would go on to lead courageously and help launch a worldwide movement that continues to this day. 33

[1] John 21:15-17 (NIV)

Join the conversation about this article

facebook facebook.com/33theseries
twitter @33theseries

Looking Back Presented by John Bryson

I. INTRODUCTION

1.   Every man has a _____.

2.   Too often, men do not know how to deal with their hurts, hopes and emotions.

II. LOOKING BACK

1.   Every guy has been shaped by the key moments in his life.

2.   Too many guys are _____ by the events in their past that they don't understand.

3.   To be a real man, you have to look back and figure out what has shaped you.

4.   We will be covering some _____ topics.

III. THREE KEY IDEAS TO GUIDE US

1. Take a _____ approach to analyzing our past.

   - Manhood Definition:

     — Reject Passivity
     — Accept Responsibility
     — Lead Courageously
     — Invest Eternally

   - We're going to take the initiative to look back on our lives.

2. The concept of _____.

   - The deepest wounds that men can experience in life aren't physical but are the wounds of his soul.

   - The natural instinct of a man who has a wounded soul is to simply _____ it's not there.

   - Some guys compensate for the pain by learning not to feel.

   - Wound: Any _____ issue where a lack of closure adversely impacts and shapes the direction and dynamics of a man's life now.

3. Ultimately, God is the _____ of your life.

    •   God can redeem your past and bless your future.

    •   "And we know that for those who love God all things work together for good, for those who are called according to his purpose." Romans 8:28 (ESV)

IV. THE EXPERTS: UNDERSTANDING THE IMPORTANCE OF OUR STORY

1. Jeff Schulte, Executive Director, Sage Hill Institute, an initiative for Authentic Christian leadership.

2. Dr. Chip Dodd, Executive Director and Co-founder of the Center for Personal Excellence, a treatment center working with high-level executives.

SESSION ONE | LOOKING BACK

DISCUSSION / REFLECTION QUESTIONS

1. Discuss with your group any hesitancy to look back at the defining moment and key relationships in your life.

2. Do you tend to blame your past or ignore your past? Why?

THE REST OF THE STORY...

A rough start doesn't have to be the final chapter in a man's story. History is littered with accounts of consequential men who suffered through painful, humiliating experiences as part of their story before enjoying their greatest triumphs. The common thread? They refused to allow their setbacks to be the end of their stories.

Bill Belichick - His five-year tenure as head coach of the Cleveland Browns was abysmal, the team posting a 36-44 record and only one playoff appearance. Belichick resigned in disgrace, but would resurrect his career as head coach of the New England Patriots, winning multiple Super Bowls and dominating the NFL.

Terry Fox - An aggressive cancer diagnosis resulted in the loss of one of his legs. Undeterred, Fox embarked on a distance run across Canada to raise awareness for cancer research. Fox eventually lost his battle to the disease, but his run inspired the world's largest ongoing one-day fund-raiser for cancer research.

John Grisham - Grisham's first novel, *A Time to Kill,* was rejected by 16 literary agents and more than 30 publishing houses before it received a positive response. Now Grisham has more than 275 million books in print in 40 languages, and nine of his novels have been made into feature films.

Abraham Lincoln - The Illinois lawyer endured a number of personal and political setbacks before his election as 16th President of the United States. He mourned the untimely deaths of his mom and girlfriend, suffered a business failure, and lost an election before his leadership helped shape the destiny of a nation.

R. H. Macy - The Massachusetts native opened four different retail stores over a twelve-year period. All four failed. His fifth attempt, R. H. Macy Dry Goods of New York City, succeeded, eventually becoming one of the world's largest department stores with more than 800 locations and $24 billion in annual revenue.

SCRIPTURE REFERENCES

Romans 8:28 (ESV) "And we know that for those who love God all things work together for good, for those who are called according to his purpose."

SUPPORTING RESOURCES

Allender, Dan. *To Be Told: God Invites You to Coauthor Your Future.* Waterbrook Press, 2005. In this book, author and counselor Dan Allender suggests that by more accurately understandingly our past we are better equipped to join God in coauthoring our future.

Dodd, Chip. *The Voice of the Heart: A Call to Full Living.* Sage Hill Resources, 2001. Dr. Chip Dodd provides a guide for understanding and navigating our emotions and experiences.

Dad

SESSION **TWO** | Training Guide

THIS SERIES CAN ALSO BE EXPERIENCED IN THE 33 APP

STANDING IN THE DARKNESS, a few steps removed from the thick, black curtain separating him from an auditorium filled with people, Daniel Beaty closes his eyes and exhales. In a moment, he will stride confidently to his mark—a small strip of gaffer's tape gripping the maple wood paneling at center stage—and bare his father wound for the audience to see.

THE WOUND, for so long a source of enormous pain in his life, is healing. It has not disappeared entirely, and possibly never will in this lifetime; but it is far enough along in its progress that Daniel willingly reveals it to others through his art, with hopes that they will be motivated to find healing for their own wounds.

It is a complex undertaking, to purge one's pain in performance halls filled with strangers. Daniel has delivered this autobiographical spoken word piece, entitled "Knock, Knock," hundreds of times before, each a fresh reminder of the boy who desperately longed for the attention and embrace of his dad. Each performance leaves him a little stronger, loosening the grip of the wounds of the past on his present and future.

by Grant Guffin

Daniel Beaty was almost born in prison. His father was a heroin dealer, and police raided the family's home when his mother was in the final stages of her pregnancy. Because of her proximity to the drugs, Daniel's mom was also arrested. To prevent her from doing jail time and to shorten the length of his own sentence, Daniel's dad agreed to a plea deal; but in doing so, he was required to provide incriminating information on his associates.

Following Daniel's birth, his mother returned to her job as a social worker, leaving his dad at home as the primary caregiver. Each morning father and son enjoyed their special game of "Knock, Knock" and other bonding activities together. Daniel specifically recalls trips to the grocery store on his dad's shoulders. Unfortunately, the closeness he felt with his dad was short lived.

"When I was three years old my father was arrested again for selling drugs," Daniel explains. "But at this point, he had started using the heroin he was selling. He said part of it was because of the tremendous amount of guilt he felt for turning in other members of his "crew" as a part of his earlier plea deal."

Daniel's dad was sentenced to eight-and-a-half years in prison this time. Eventually, Daniel and his mom made the trek to the correctional facility. For the first time in his life, Daniel was face-to-face with the man he loved dearly but unable to leap into his arms as he'd always done. **"It was a painful experience** for us both, and my father made my mother promise to never bring me to see him again while he was in prison," Daniel says.

"I had a huge wound that was created because my father was a loving and charismatic man and he was my principal caregiver. Now he was gone. But not only was he gone, he forbade my mother to bring me to see him. As a result of that, there was an emptiness; there was a sadness. There was a pervasive sense of abandonment that became very big in my life and heart and mind."

To make matters worse, Daniel's brother, ten years his elder, developed an addiction to crack cocaine. Refusing to give up on him, their mom decided to allow him to remain in the home. While she was away at work, Daniel would often be left alone with his brother, who sometimes turned violent toward him.

"A lot of fear was created and it compounded the idea that I could not rely on the men in my life," Daniel confesses. "They were going to be hurtful people and that was who I was destined to become."

But Daniel would discover a different path for himself. While watching archive footage of Dr. Martin Luther King Jr.'s "I Have A Dream" speech, Daniel took special notice of the impact one man's words could have on so many. Through the mentoring of a teacher, Daniel cultivated an interest in public speaking, and soon found himself addressing crowds at local school and community events.

"I saw a vision of myself as an adult in an amphitheater speaking or performing, doing some type of huge presentation in front of numbers of people," he explains. "And it gave me a sense of peace; it gave me a sense of vision that there was something better than the chaos that I was living."

Daniel soared as both an academic and an artist, winning one of Yale's top honors and leading his class in graduation exercises. But his father wound continued to fester. "There was a void I didn't understand and I was looking for things to fill it," he says. "There was a concept that I was not good, that I was unlovable, that I did not have worth, and that no matter how much I achieved I could not make myself feel like I mattered."

Watch Daniel Beaty knock, knock in session 2.

Daniel realized that much of his unhappiness was rooted in a father wound that desperately needed healing.

He decided to take the first step by reaching out: "I wrote him letters while he was in prison and I expressed my hurt and my rage. He wrote me letters back apologizing, making excuses for his behavior."

The letters marked the beginning of a ten-year journey to healing that involved a number of visits, painful conversations and ultimately forgiveness. Daniel says it wasn't easy, a path marked by "a lot of resistance...and rage and disappointment, but I can say that there has been a deliverance around it because I have authentic joy. I still have the range of emotions around it, but I can now say that I have true joy and happiness and I have it in a sustained way that I didn't think was ever going to be possible."

"I had to discover that I am my father's son but I'm not his choices," Daniel explains. It was important for Daniel to heal this relationship, but this particular man was the product of the choices he had made. "I stand in faith for my father's healing."

Daniel hopes that other men who are suffering with father wounds will benefit from his experiences: "As men we're taught we need to be strong and tough, but that too often causes us to cover our pain rather than deal with it. We're more likely to pass that pain on if we haven't allowed God to heal it. As a leader of a family, you're responsible for what your family inherits...your children, grandchildren and beyond your lifetime. Letting God deal with us around father issues can break cycles that can impact the future."

Daniel's wound is now a scar. The mark is there, but it no longer causes him shame. "There is still pain, but it isn't a pain that debilitates me. It's a pain that's a reservoir I can dig into to be a source of passion and inspiration. I can speak from it, and tears and passion and emotion can be present, but it isn't emotion that hurts me. It's emotion that can be used to communicate the message with passion so that they get it." **33**

Join the conversation about this article

facebook facebook.com/33theseries
twitter @33theseries

33 THE SERIES

33 Presenter Insight

Unremarkable

by Tierce Green, 33 Presenter

Our neighbors picked me up from school that day - a day that would become a defining moment for me just a few weeks after my tenth birthday. Our house was packed with an odd mix of relatives and neighbors. My mom guided me through the crowd and into my room. With courage and compassion she did her best to explain that my dad had been in an accident. He would not be coming home. He was gone.

I remember the tears, but what was I crying about? My father had never really been a dad to me. In my short life, he had been virtually invisible. I didn't really know what a dad was; I just knew that I didn't have one anymore. Years later, I learned how my mom had shielded me from his excessive drinking and his abusive tendencies. I guess it was a good thing that he was distant and disconnected from me.

There is a word I use to describe an experience that is just so-so. Unremarkable. That was my dad. My experience with him was not unpleasant. It was just unremarkable. I honestly cannot remember the sound of his voice. At best, he is just a blur.

I only have one family photo with my dad in it. We're at my sister's wedding. It looks as if he's been attached to the group – an awkward fit. We could Photoshop him out without having to change any of the details of that event. His presence there and at other events was inconsequential. Unremarkable.

I didn't fully appreciate it at the time, but looking back over the years, I could see the strength God gave my mom to raise a headstrong son like me. She prayed hard that God would cross my path with men

"There must be a time when a man draws a line that defines what was then and what is now."

who would fill the void left by my dad and show me what it meant to be a man.

Like most young men who grow up without a father, I guessed about a lot of things. For example, I guessed in my relationships with girls and in the way I managed my money. I grappled with manhood and what life is about. Most of the time I guessed wrong and just gave in to the culture.

But God answered my mom's prayers. In my teenage years, there were men like my brother-in-law who modeled for me what it meant to be a man, a husband and a son. In my twenties, there were others who showed me what it meant to be a father to their sons and how to lead in their homes.

It's easy to take shots at a dad who was

disengaged, and it's convenient to use the void left by his death as an excuse for irresponsibility. There must be a time, however, when a man draws a line that defines what was then and what is now. *There must be a defining moment when he decides, regardless of what he has or hasn't been given, that he is going to reject the natural passivity he was born with and the cultural passivity he has been conditioned with.* There must be a time when he accepts responsibility and makes a decision to lead courageously, or at best he will only be a blur. Not necessarily a bad husband or father, just unremarkable. **33**

Just Like

by Lecrae

The following lyrics are a portion of Lecrae's song, *Just Like You*, featured in the session video, demonstrating the powerful impact an absent father can have on his son.

I was created by God
But I ain't wanna be like Him
I wanna be Him
The Jack Sparrow of my Caribbean
I remember the first created being
And how he shifted the blame on his dame
From fruit he shouldn't have eaten
And now look at us all out of Eden
Wearing designer fig leaves by Louis Vuitton
Make believe it
But God sees through my foolish pride
And how I'm weak like Adam
Another victim of Lucifer's lies

But then in steps Jesus
All men were created to lead
But we need somebody to lead us
More than a teacher
But somebody to buy us back
From the darkness
You say that He redeemed us
Taught us that real leaders follow God
Finish the work 'cause we're on our job
Taught us not to rob
But give life, love a wife
Like He loved the Church
Not seeing how many hearts we can break first

I wanna be like you in every way
So if I gotta die everyday
Unworthy sacrifice
But the least I can do is give the most of me
Because being just like you
Is what I'm 'spose to be
They say you came for the lame, I'm the lamest
I made a mess but you'll say you'll erase it
I'll take it
You said you came for the lame, I'm the lamest
I broke my life
But you say you'll replace it
I'll take it

I just wanna be like you
Walk like, talk like, even think like you
The only one I could look to
You're teaching me to be just like you
Well I just gotta be like
I just gotta be like you

Dad Presented by Tierce Green

I. THE IMPORTANCE OF FATHERS

1. Present or _____, good or bad, the father/son relationship is significant in shaping all of us.

2. None of us were raised by a perfect father and this has left all of us wounded to one degree or another.

3. "Grandchildren are the crown of old men, And the **glory of sons is their fathers**." Proverbs 17:6 (NASB)

4. Every father gets undeserved _____ from his son the minute he comes into the world.

5. Today in the United States, _____ of children grow up apart from their biological fathers.

6. Modern research has demonstrated the importance of fathers:

- Statistically, children growing up in father-absent homes are more likely to:

    - Die in infancy
    - Live in poverty
    - End up in prison
    - Use drugs
    - Be abused
    - Be overweight
    - Dropout of school

- Children with involved fathers are more likely to have:

    - Better grades
    - Better verbal skills
    - More confidence
    - Better physical health

- Recent research indicates that fathers _____ add value to their children.

Sources: *Father Facts 6* (National Fatherhood Initiative, 2011); Jeffrey Rosenberg and W. Bradford Wilcox, *The Importance of Fathers in the Healthy Development of Children* (U.S. Department of Health and Human Services, 2006).

II. DEFINITIONS AND REMEMBERING DAD

1. Wound: Any unresolved issue where a lack of closure adversely impacts and shapes the direction and dynamics of a man's life now.

2. Father Wound: It's "an ongoing emotional, social, or spiritual deficit that's caused by the lack of a healthy _____ with dad and now must be overcome by other means."

3. It was caused when there was a lack of heart connection, or companionship or substantive direction from dad.

4. It's about how your dad _____ to you.

III. THREE COMMON RESPONSES TO THE FATHER WOUND

1. Anger and pain

    •   The Bible shows a connection between a man's _____ and his dad.

    •   "Fathers, do not provoke your children to anger, but bring them up in the discipline and instruction of the Lord." Ephesians 6:4 (ESV)

    •   "Fathers, do not provoke your children, or they may lose heart." Colossians 3:21 (NRSV)

    •   Without a dad, there is a _____ in a son's life and part of what fills that vacuum is rage.

2. The bottling up of feelings

    •   To _____ like you're not affected.

    •   You can never completely bottle it up, it'll express itself somehow.

    •   According to John Sowers in the *Fatherless Generation*, "Fatherlessness creates an appetite in the soul that _____ fulfillment."

- Unhealthy ways this hunger can find it's way to the surface:

    ○ Addictions or obsessions
    ○ Drugs, pornography and excessive alcohol
    ○ Performance

3. An inner sense of lostness or incompleteness.

    - Incompleteness can be _____, we never felt accepted or validated by dad.

    - Incompleteness can be _____. Dad didn't teach us to shave or balance a checking account or how to pursue a woman, etc.

IV. OVERCOMING THE EFFECTS OF THE FATHER WOUND

1. The absence of a great father is not insurmountable.

2. With Christ's help we can _____ any obstacle.

v. WHAT EVERY SON NEEDS FROM DAD

1. _____ together

2. Life skills

3. Direction with solid answers to the _____ questions of life

4. Deep life convictions

    - You will leave in your son what you have _____ out in your home.

5. Dad's heart

    - I love you
    - I'm proud of you
    - I'm affirming you

DISCUSSION / REFLECTION QUESTIONS

1.   How do you feel about your relationship with your dad? What are three words or phrases that sum up your relationship with him?

2.   This session talked about the father wound expressing itself in three ways: (1) anger and pain, (2) the bottling up of feelings, and (3) a sense of relational or informational incompleteness. Elaborate on how any of these three things describe you.

CLASSIC FATHER-SON MOVIES

Life Is Beautiful - Guido Orefice, an Italian Jew, is imprisoned with his wife and son in a Nazi concentration camp. Guido's outlook in the face of death and his selfless love for his family is a moving picture of fatherhood at its best.

Field of Dreams - Farmer Ray Kinsella builds a baseball diamond in an Iowa cornfield, unleashing a magical portal to the past. Kinsella sets out on a quest to ease the pain of a mystery figure. Tears will form in the driest eyes when Ray and his dad play catch at movie's end.

The Godfather - The Best Picture Award winner of 1972 portrays the relationship of Don Vito Corleone, head of a prominent organized crime family and his son Michael. The film greatly demonstrates the power of a father's influence in a son's life, good or bad.

Finding Nemo - Don't underestimate the power of this animated story that portrays the limitless love of a father toward his son. Marlin's efforts to rescue Nemo are at times hilarious and other times moving. Marlin's growth as a character is noteworthy as he learns to "let go."

the RED ZONE

Star Wars Episode VI: Return of the Jedi - This epic space adventure pits the forces of the dark side and one of its villians, Darth Vader, against Vader's son, Luke Skywalker. Vader finds there is good in his heart when faced with the possibility of watching his son be murdered by evil Emperor Palpatine.

Indiana Jones and the Last Crusade - Legendary archaeologist Jones tracks down his father, who has been kidnapped by the Nazis. The two join forces to battle Hitler's henchmen and capture the Holy Grail of Christ. The chemistry between father and son makes for several memorable exchanges.

Pursuit of Happyness - The real-life story of Chris Gardner, a single father and businessman whose decisions render him and his young son homeless. Chris calls upon every ounce of effort and ingenuity he can muster to change his circumstances, demonstrating the desire of a father to provide for his son.

The Champ - Down-and-out boxer Billy Flynn works to make a life for his son, returning to the ring against doctor's orders. The boy's mom, who abandoned father and son for her new millionaire husband, wants the boy back. The film's climax is gut wrenching.

SCRIPTURE REFERENCES

Proverbs 17:6 (NASB) "Grandchildren are the crown of old men, and the glory of sons is their fathers."

Ephesians 6:4 (ESV) "Fathers, do not provoke your children to anger, but bring them up in the discipline and instruction of the Lord."

Colossians 3:21 (NRSV) "Fathers, do not provoke your children, or they may lose heart."

Philippians 3:12-13 (NET) "Not that I have already attained this – that is, I have not already been perfected – but I strive to lay hold of that for which Christ Jesus also laid hold of me. Brothers and sisters, I do not consider myself to have attained this. Instead I am single-minded. Forgetting the things that are behind and reaching out for the things that are ahead."

SUPPORTING RESOURCES

Miller, Donald. *Father Fiction: Chapters for a Fatherless Generation.* Howard Books, 2010. In this mainly autobiographical account, author Donald Miller recounts his experience with fatherlessness and the affects it had on him.

Sowers, John. *Fatherless Generation: Redeeming the Story.* Zondervan, 2010. John Sowers, president of The Mentoring Project, discusses the ramifications of fatherlessness for today's youth.

Father Facts 6. National Fatherhood Initiative. 2011. The most complete and comprehensive collection of data on the causes and consequences of father absence.

Mom

SESSION **THREE** | Training Guide

THIS SERIES CAN ALSO BE EXPERIENCED IN THE **33** APP

I ♥ MOM

BY BRIAN JONES

The wise man pursues knowledge. The pursuit of knowledge may lead a man to science, medicine, philosophy or to any number of life-changing experiences.

This is the story of one man's pursuit for knowledge and a mom's love that changed him forever. More than anything, he desired to be a scholar, one who was famous for his reasoning and intellect. This man was respected by his peers and pedagogues alike.

Behind his academic prowess, however, there was a selfish desire to obtain personal happiness and pleasure. Any energy that was left after his academic studies was focused entirely on enjoying the pleasures of the flesh. A beautiful woman would catch his eye and he could not control his lust and sexual desires. As far as he was concerned, women were only good for "one thing."

After years of seeking empty pleasures, he began to grow weary of his shallow lifestyle. He was disillusioned with himself and his wicked ways. There was a disconnect in his soul, an uneasy feeling that his life was in need of drastic change. He began to ask himself- why am I living like this?

THE POWER OF A SPIRITUAL MOM IN A SON'S LIFE

REAL MEN

In his search for answers and redemption, he came face to face with something unexpected along the way - his heritage. This man's past was fragmented and disjointed. Although his father was well-respected in the community, he lacked any sense of principle and was utterly immoral, setting a less than desirable model for his young son.

His mother was the complete opposite. A spiritually strong woman, she was deeply convicted about the world's injustices and was relentless in her faith. She did everything she could to instill nobility and goodness in her son, believing that he would find a life filled with purpose. Unfortunately, for most of her lifetime, he chose to model his actions after his father's sinful example. Time and time again, choice after choice, he slipped into his sexual desires.

As he began to turn from his hedonistic pursuits, this man tried to settle down with one woman.

A LOVING MOM CAN BE ONE OF A SON'S GREATEST BLESSINGS

LOVE MOM

She loved him deeply, gave birth to his only child-a son, but his father's influence had poisoned how he related to women, and he constantly struggled with how to love her, and only her. Fueled by frustration, he finally resolved that if he could not manage his desires, he would abstain from women entirely, and ultimately chose a life of celibacy.

The years passed, filled primarily with academia and a constant pursuit for reconciliation. His father passed away, and though his negative presence was gone, the examples he had set for his son remained. On a cool summer day, desperate to be free of his inner demons, this man stopped fighting, and surrendered himself completely to God...the God his mother had spent a lifetime directing him to. His heart was changed. Now, instead of living a life lashing out at his mom he established a new relationship with her. In addition to restoring a healthy relationship with his mom it also improved his relationships with women in general. A relationship with Christ helped restore his relationship with his mother. He later shared his whole story in his *Confessions*. Now, Augustine and his mother, Monica, are both considered Christian saints. 33

Join the conversation about this article

facebook facebook.com/33theseries

twitter @33theseries

33 **Presenter Insight**

Bryan Carter

What Did She Say?

by Brian Jones

Bryan Carter came into the world as a sickly child. He was blessed to have two loving parents that cared for him deeply. His mother was well equipped for the task, as she was a nurse by profession. Unfortunately, the job tied her up during the day and she was unable to spend as much time with her son. Bryan did not have many opportunities to connect with her; she was commonly gone. Bryan recalls, "my relationship with my mom was not a strong relationship. In fact, my grandma played a more important part of raising me than my mom did."

Even though his relationship was not strong with his mom, that didn't mean that his mom didn't have a strong personality. In fact, her strong personality came from her mom. Bryan grew up in a family where the women were not only strong, but sometimes controlling. These women were loose cannons and not many people would stand up to them. His grandmother lived quite the life; she was never just on the cart, she drove the cart. Bryan recalls, "My grandmother is very demanding. There are big consequences if you don't do what she wants."

When Bryan was introducing his wife to his grandmother, an unfortunate encounter ensued. Over breakfast, his grandmother made a derogatory comment about his bride. His grandmother blurted out in a crass and tactless manner. Both Bryan and his wife were left speechless, they didn't know what to do. On the drive home, his wife said, "I'm done."

Bryan and his wife would not see his grandmother for years. It wasn't until he was about to be installed at his church did his grandmother make an effort to see him again. Bryan knew that he needed to hold her accountable. The interaction between he, his wife and his grandmother could not be the same as the first. He needed to step up and confront her. Bryan drove to the bus stop to pick her up. He said, "Grandma, you really hurt my wife's feelings. You need to apologize to her the next time you see her." For the first time, Bryan confronted one of the strong women in his life. What transpired next, shocked him. His grandmother said, "I will apologize. What I said was mean."

Bryan now teaches men how to deal with a controlling mother-figure. Men have to be confident in who they are and need to be comfortable in speaking with the women in their lives. Men cannot be passive, they have to stand up for what's right. Bryan declares, "Sometimes that involves standing up for your wife, protecting her and insuring that others honor her." While Bryan confesses that he used to be passive and would just "write-off" what his grandmother would say, the dysfunction he had adapted to was not right. Expectations needed to be changed.

Bryan's relationship with his grandmother is now better because he took the initiative to deal with the wound he had head-on. When a man takes the initiative and exerts courage to deal with his mother-wounds, that man becomes a better example to his family and the men in his life. 33

How to develop a plan to overcome the mother wound:

- **Address specific issues**
  Don't be vague, or general

- **Establish boundaries for future interactions**
  Draw time-tested boundaries that dictate how both of you will interact

- **Spell out clear consequences for violating boundaries**
  Let her know the cost of crossing the established boundaries

Join the conversation about this article

facebook facebook.com/33theseries
twitter @33theseries

Mom Presented by Bryan Carter

I. THE INFLUENCE OF A MOM

1. The mother/son _____ is an important part of who you are.

2. The way your mom "has handled your needs as a child has shaped your worldview, your relationships, your marriage, your career, your self-image, your life. What we learned in our relationship with our mother deeply affects every area of our adult life." - *The Mom Factor*, by Henry Cloud

II. TWO SIGNIFICANT BREAKS WITH MOM

- A healthy relationship with mom requires two significant breaks.

3. There must be a _____ separation from mom at birth to end the oneness that began at conception.

4. There must be an _____ separation from mom when a boy transitions to manhood.

   - Many men are left deeply entrenched or _____ connected to mom.

   - Men who are overly connected to mom can feel like their masculinity is _____.

   - "Therefore a man shall LEAVE his father and his mother and HOLD FAST to his wife and they shall become one flesh." Genesis 2:24 (ESV)

III. THE MOTHER WOUND AND ITS EFFECTS

1. Mother Wound: "An _____, emotional relationship with mom that causes a son to either be threatened by the influence of women later on in life or to overidentify and become submissive to the influence of women. "

2. Men with a mother wound will often drift to one of two extremes in how they relate to women. They often become either DOMINANT MALES or SOFT MALES.

    *   Dominant males: too _____ towards women

    *   Soft males: become _____ and submissive toward women

IV. COMMON CHARACTERISTICS OF THE MOTHER WOUND

1. Usually, the mother wound is not one of inattention but overattention.

2. This wound often begins with an absent or distant _____.

3. Marion Levy writes that modern men "are overwhelmingly likely to have been reared under the direct domination and supervision of females from birth to maturity."

V. FOUR TYPES OF MOMS THAT CONTRIBUTE TO THE MOTHER WOUND

1. The _____ Mom

    •   She stays oblivious to her son's need to connect with other men and to make a healthy break with her.

2. The Hurting Mom

    •   A woman who has lost emotional connection with her husband and she makes up for this by over-connecting to her son.

3. The Unwilling-to-_____ Mom

    •   Oftentimes, these moms have dominant personalities and they simply love to be in control.

4. The Fill-in-the-_____ Mom

    •   This can lead to over-connection and dependence if the son doesn't have strong male mentors to guide him.

VI. JESUS AND HIS MOM

1. Did you know that Jesus had some _____ with his mom?

2. "Then Jesus entered a house, and again a crowd gathered, so that he and his disciples were not even able to eat. When his family heard about it, they went to take charge of him, for they said 'He is out of his mind'... Then Jesus' mother and brothers arrived. Standing outside, they sent someone in to call him. A crowd was sitting around him and they told him, 'Your mother and brothers are outside looking for you.' 'Who are my mother and my brothers?' he asked. Then he looked at those seated in a circle around him and said, 'Here are my mother and my brothers! Whoever does God's will is my brother and sister and mother.'" Mark 3:20-21; 31-35 (NIV)

    *   Jesus had healthy _____ with his mom.

3. "Near the cross of Jesus stood his mother... When Jesus saw his mother there, and the disciple whom he loved standing nearby, he said to his mother, 'Dear woman, here is your son' and to the disciple, 'Here is your mother.' From that time on, this disciple took her into his home." John 19:25-27 (NIV)

    *   Jesus' actions respected her role as mom.

4. Jesus offers us a perfect example of how to interact with our moms:

    •   Healthy boundaries

    •   Genuine love

    •   Proper respect

5. Many of us have _____ business with mom.

DISCUSSION / REFLECTION QUESTIONS

1. Describe your relationship with your mom growing up. How is (was) it as an adult?

2. Would you say that you have effectively made "the break" with mom? Does your mom presently exert an unhealthy influence in your life? Your marriage? What would your wife say?

3. Can you see a connection between the way you relate to your mom and how you relate to other women in your life?

AUTHENTIC MANHOOD

YOUR STRATEGIC MOVE

Some men may want to write a letter to mom that initiates the conversation about a redefined relationship. If so, below is a sample to help you get started.

Mom,

You are amazing in so many ways and I am so glad that you are my mom! You've always been there for me, been one of my biggest fans and always believed in me. I wouldn't be who I am today without your love, support, encouragement and guidance.

While I will always want and need you in my life, the time has come for me to become my own man. Because you have always been there, I have come to rely on you too much. When I lived at home as a boy, I absolutely needed and welcomed your guidance. But now I'm out on my own, it's time for me to stand on my own two feet and chase my own dreams, and maybe even make my own mistakes.

Here's what I would like to ask of you as we move forward...

MOM'S THE

In more than 60 years of television sitcoms, a handful of overbearing "mom" characters have transcended their presence on the small screen to find a permanent place in pop culture. At times endearing and other times infuriating, each of these fictional moms are guilty of loving those around them a little too much.

Clair Huxtable, *The Cosby Show*
"I would like to know what we ever asked you to do except hang up your clothes before they take root."

Claire Dunphy, *Modern Family*
"Sweetheart, I would love to be wrong, but I don't live with the right people for that."

WORD!

Edith Bunker, *All in the Family*
"That's right Mike, if at first you don't succeed, try, try again."

Mabel Thomas, *What's Happening!*
"Roger...give me your belt."

Marie Barone, *Everybody Loves Raymond*
"Your father...his idea of culture is an undershirt with sleeves."

Lois Wilkerson, *Malcolm in the Middle*
"Look, Reese. Some people are born book-smart. Others are born crafty and street-smart. You, I'm afraid, are neither."

SCRIPTURE REFERENCES

Genesis 2:24 (ESV) "Therefore a man shall leave his father and his mother and hold fast to his wife, and they shall become one flesh."

Mark 3:20-21 (NIV) "Then Jesus entered a house, and again a crowd gathered, so that he and his disciples were not even able to eat. When his family heard about this, they went to take charge of him, for they said, "He is out of his mind.""

Mark 3:31-35 (NIV) "Then Jesus' mother and brothers arrived. Standing outside, they sent someone in to call him. A crowd was sitting around him, and they told him, 'Your mother and brothers are outside looking for you.' 'Who are my mother and my brothers?' he asked. Then he looked at those seated in a circle around him and said, 'Here are my mother and my brothers! Whoever does God's will is my brother and sister and mother.'"

John 19:25-27 (ESV) "But standing by the cross of Jesus were his mother and his mother's sister, Mary the wife of Clopas, and Mary Magdalene. When Jesus saw his mother and the disciple whom he loved standing nearby, he said to his mother, 'Woman, behold, your son!' Then he said to the disciple, 'Behold, your mother!' And from that hour the disciple took her to his own home."

SUPPORTING RESOURCES

Cloud, Henry and John Townsend. *The Mom Factor.* Zondervan, 1996. Christian psychologists Henry Cloud and John Townsend discuss the potential effects of a mom on a son.

Meeker, Meg. *Boys Will Be Boys: 7 Secrets to Raising Healthy Sons.* Ballantine Books, 2009. Medical doctor, Meg Meeker, offers advice on how to raise boys. Chapter seven, "A Mother's Son," is especially insightful.

SESSION 4

Healing

SESSION **FOUR** | Training Guide

THIS SERIES CAN ALSO BE EXPERIENCED IN THE **33** APP

trading in

WHAT ~~HURTS~~ FOR

"So here I am: ~~a high school drop out~~ with a 4.0 GPA in college; ~~an ex-con~~ healed from my past with the opportunity to travel the world and rub elbows with outstanding people in the community; a waiter at a restaurant and working part-time at a great church. I'm a ~~jacked up, broken, formally drug-addicted poor excuse of a~~ man who now makes a life <u>trying to help people just as wicked as I am.</u>"

A week before Mother's Day, a nun who volunteered in a prison filled a box with cards. She hoped inmates would write their moms. They emptied the box in a matter of hours. A month later she replenished it for Father's Day. No cards were touched. Jason Duncan never served time in that prison. But until he faced his wounds, he too would have skipped out on a note to his dad.

"Let me start by saying I haven't done much in my life that I'm proud of. I've been a negative influence on everyone and everything around me. So God wrecked me - or should I say, he allowed me to wreck my life. I was 18 when my parents divorced. I dropped out of school and started working at a restaurant...the gateway to my own personal hell."

Much in life knocked Jason on his back. Born in California, Jason never lived in one place very long. His dad served in the Navy. They moved around like nomads along the west coast from one duty station to the next.

Just as his voice started changing octaves, he suffered a blow. His mom was diagnosed with multiple sclerosis. At the time, dad was serving Uncle Sam on a six month tour at sea. Before Jason graduated from junior high, he became man of the house. Mom couldn't cook or clean anymore. Rather than run the bases after school, Jason ran for groceries. Instead of playing outside, Jason started paying the bills. As Jason adjusted to his new normal, dad came home and told the family it was time to ship off again. This time they were moving to the other coast – the beaches of North Carolina.

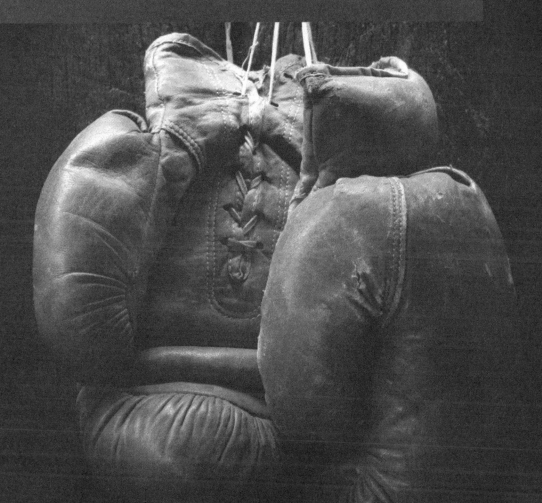

WHAT HEALS

Written by Brian Goins

"So here my brother and I were, the new kids in school yet again, but this time with California surfer accents, further setting us apart from our peers," Jason remembers. "I was wrestling with this, with going through puberty, with my responsibilities to a sick mother and family, trying to discover who I was, and just wanting to blend in."

When dad wasn't on duty with the Navy, he found other ways to slip away from his family. He worked on a double masters and took on a second job as a waiter. Jason recalls, "He said it was to pay the bills, but I think it was just so he didn't have to be around."

Once his parents split up, Jason ran away from his wounds. He dropped out of high school and landed a job at a restaurant. There he ran into James the bartender. Without a clear definition of manhood, boys will settle for any model: "James had a decent house with a couple guys for roommates, a nice car, threw a party just about every night of the week, and always had a couple of hot girls fighting over him. I decided I wanted to be that guy. I set on the path of earthly pleasure, and over the next decade I accomplished my goal."

Jason developed his own definition of manhood. **Women were toys, friends were used and Jason quickly found ways to medicate his pain from his childhood wounds.**

"I became a bartender. I became an expert at throwing house parties. I became a street racer. I became a full blown alcoholic and drug addict." When dad did resurface from time to time he only offered observations, "My father

Jason developed his own definition of manhood, one based on instant gratification.

called me a cyclone of destruction" Jason said.

"Because of the lifestyle I was leading, I started getting into trouble with the law. It began with speeding tickets. Half the time I didn't even show up for court. My solution was to modify cars to outrun the cops. I graduated from speeding tickets to reckless endangerment, evading arrest, excessive speeding and operating illegal vehicles."

After losing the "girl of his dreams," Jason numbed his pain on a frat-like binge. Within a week he lost his job, wrecked his car in a street race and was thrown in jail.

"I ran out of tears and reached that state of numb disconnectedness. Out of sheer boredom I opened the Bible randomly, and it fell open to Deuteronomy 28:30, 'You shall betroth a wife, but another man shall ravish her. You shall build a house, but you shall not dwell in it. You shall plant a vineyard, but you shall not enjoy its fruit.'"

God spoke to Jason through the Bible. Jason saw his lifestyle, like a cyclone that had ripped up his vineyard. In that moment, he realized God was very much alive and active...at least while he was behind bars.

"I got out of jail about a week later, and the first thing I did was buy some weed and a beer. I continued life as if nothing had happened there in that cell. I changed only one thing: I started to pray, primarily for God to help me move away from my addictions."

After a party in North Carolina, Jason was pulled over for drunk driving. The arresting officer ran his name and discovered Jason had skipped out on probation for a crime he committed while visiting his mom four years previous. They shipped him back home and sentenced Jason to two years in a minimum-security facility. That's when God started answering his prayers.

Getting off the Ground

After six weeks in prison, about 50 of the 570 inmates were called into a meeting. "We were told that a new program was being launched that would allow some of us to attend college, on a real campus, with real students, for real college credit. Only ten would be chosen out of 1,500." Jason volunteered. After an intensive testing and interviewing process, Jason was accepted.

They designed the program to help inmates earn a living and learn how to live when they left prison. Jason was required to go through Alcoholics Anonymous. "At the time I had no desire to be sober! I discovered to my surprise that the 12 steps do in fact work and I found something I had been craving my whole life: community, connection, and acceptance." In addition to the weekly AA meetings, **Jason attended a 24-week course called the Quest for Authentic Manhood (Men's Fraternity).** **"I learned what a man is and does." He found Jesus the carpenter a much better model to follow than James the bartender.**

The felon tasted freedom behind bars. Jason realized, "God's plan for me, even if it meant prison, was better than any plan I could come up with myself."

Putting down the gloves

"Are you a convicted felon?" Imagine answering yes to that question on every job application, rental agreement, or date. Jason learned that facing your wounds requires responsibility. **He discovered the best healing for your wounds is simply sharing your pain.** "It's been my experience that those who have been most dependent upon God have the most difficult stories to tell."

After Jason finished prison, he picked up a pen and wrote the man who shipped in and out of his life - dad. It had been years since they had talked. In a jail cell, Jason started writing. He didn't berate him or tear him down. Jason found ways to praise him, honor him, and express his desire to start fresh. Jason apologized for how his anger sabotaged their relationship.

"We have a saying in AA," Jason says, "Keep your side of the street clean." Own your stuff and let God deal with their stuff. He encourages these men to write without expecting affection from dad. "The other party's response doesn't matter. Go slow. Don't expect a lot right away. Tell them how you feel. Tell them all you wanted to hear was 'I love you...I'm proud of you,' and let God deal with their heart."

"Tell them all you wanted to hear was 'I love you...I'm proud of you,' and let God deal with their heart."

Today, Jason celebrates the small wins with dad, like taking him out of the apartment for a baseball game. His dad fights depression and battles the bottle. But Jason loves his dad anyway. The formally absent father has an ever-present son.

Though Jason still works as a waiter, he spends most of his free time working on a degree in international business. The former dropout carries a 4.0 GPA and dreams of taking the Gospel to third world countries.

Life dealt a blow to Jason, but God healed him. A major part of his healing was dealing with that deep gash in his heart caused by his own father wound. Without doing the hard work of mending the relationship with his dad, Jason's healing would never be complete. Now that the wound has been healed, Jason helps guide other men to deal with their own wounds and brings them to the Healer. Jason doesn't mind sharing his scars. He's gone from felon to free man, alcoholic to ambassador, maniac to missionary, wounded son to healed man who understands the needs of his own heart. ⅗

33 Presenter Insight

Feeling is Healing

by James Pecht

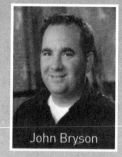

John Bryson

Many adults consider it an insult to be told they behave like 4-year-olds. John Bryson considers it a compliment.

The reason? Little kids don't put masks on their feelings.
"I don't ever wonder what my 4-year-old wants. He is always in-tune with what he wants to do at any given moment," John says. "Somewhere along the way, society has taught us to detach from our hearts."

That detachment is a real problem, and it's a common reaction to the wounds of the past. John knows the consequences all too well.
"I spent the first 35 years of my life undervaluing interpersonal relationships and not developing emotional fluency or emotional currency," he says. "I accomplished more by my 30s than I ever dreamed possible, but inside I was a mess and disconnected because I had forgotten how to feel."

Bryson says feelings are the currency that connect people to God, their spouses, their children and their friends. *In order to heal from your wounds, you must be willing to embrace your emotions.*

"I was a typical friendless American male. I knew everyone, but nobody knew me. And they surely didn't know what was going on under the hood of my life because I didn't know what was going on under the hood of my life."

For a lot of men, it's easier to lead and relate from their minds or from their hands. They're good at making empirical decisions and taking action, but they have no idea how to feel. John says fathers often don't show much emotion in front of their sons, and they teach their sons not to cry or show emotion in public. These father wounds can be difficult to heal.

But to truly relate to God and to those around us, we must take the time to feel our emotions.

"God mentions our heart more than anything else in scripture," John says. "We're designed to feel. I think the pathway to fulfillment will not be in mere external accomplishments or successes; I think it's going to be an internal reconnection."

John says God intends for us to heal, and as such, our emotions may come out whether we want them to or not.

"That's why we have mid-life crises and why we see men do absolutely stupid things to blow up their lives," he says. "For a lot of men, that's the first time they've actually felt."

Thankfully, John didn't wait to become self-destructive before embracing his emotions. He credits his wife and some close mentors with giving him the encouragement to reconnect with his heart.

"I'm grateful for those God has put into my life, giving me the patience and grace to help me redevelop my heart and learn how to feel." 33

Join the conversation about this article

facebook facebook.com/33theseries
twitter @33theseries

Buddy Griffin

by James Pecht

It took him more than 60 years, but Buddy Griffin finally learned that a hug held far more power than a fist.

Griffin grew up in a tough and violent home. His father was both physically and verbally abusive toward him and seldom gave him encouragement.

"My dad grew up during the depression era. He was a workaholic and was very tough on me," Griffin said. "He beat me. He knocked me out more than once with his fist."

Griffin said that his upbringing understandably created a strained relationship with his father. "We were okay to be around each other, but there was never

this deep wonderful feeling of having a father," he said.

When Griffin's mother died and his father's health began to deteriorate, Griffin found himself the primary caregiver for a man he didn't like.

"I did it begrudgingly. I didn't feel comfortable doing it," he said.

That resentment could have followed Griffin for years. But a chance encounter with Robert Lewis, author of the *Quest for Authentic Manhood*, began to turn things around.

Griffin met Lewis at a conference and

> ## "Go back to wherever your father is and go tell him that you need to be hugged, and he needs to tell you that he loves you."

quickly realized the two had similar stories about their fathers. Lewis challenged him to make a change.

"Are you going to stand over that casket some day and bury that man with all that hate in your heart?" Lewis asked. "Go back to wherever your father is and go tell him that you need to be hugged, and he needs to tell you that he loves you."

Griffin was skeptical. How could the man who frequently hit and berated him suddenly change his tune? But no matter the odds, Griffin was determined to try.

He visited his father in the nursing home. "Dad, you never told me, ever, that you loved me," he said. "Will you tell me that, please?"

His father responded, "Well, I love everybody." Then, visibly uncomfortable with the situation, he got up to leave.

Griffin grabbed his father's shoulder. "Please tell me," he said. "Will you just hug me, please?"

"Well, I'm leaving," was the response.

Undeterred, Griffin came back. The same scene played itself out week after week.

After about seven weeks, Griffin's father calmly looked at him and said, "Let's do our thing." And for the first time ever, Griffin's father gave him a real hug and kissed him on the cheek.

"He told me that he loved me and just held my hand," Griffin said.

Griffin and his father continued their visits. A couple of years later, his father died – while holding Griffin's hand.

"The wonderful thing about this is that Jesus Christ had invaded our lives," Griffin said. "We had reconciliation."

And Griffin found peace in his heart.

"The day will come that I'll take my last breath, and I'm going to step over into heaven and be reunited with my dad and mom," he said. And instead of carrying on resentment and anger, "we'll have eternity to celebrate." 33

Healing Presented by John Bryson

I. INTRODUCTION

1. We are going to provide some practical advice that will help you deal with your own personal situation.

II. FIVE GUIDELINES FOR DEALING WITH WOUNDS

1. If you've been wounded by mom or dad, you've got to choose to deal with this wound _____.

    - Regardless of mom or dad's role in the situation, the burden ultimately falls on you to resolve the situation in your own life.

2. If you've been wounded by mom or dad, you should begin the process of _____.

    - You decide to no longer exact punishment in any form or fashion.

3. If you have been negatively impacted by mom or dad, _____ your story with some trustworthy men.

    - Dealing with wounds is a process.

4. If you're married and you've got _____ issues from your past, tell your wife.

5. If there are unresolved issues with a parent, this may mean that you need to have a direct but respectful conversation with mom and dad.

III. DIRECT CONVERSATIONS WITH DAD AND MOM

1. If you're a son wounded by dad, consider seeking _____ reconciliation with your father.

    *   You have to be the one to initiate.

    *   You can't control his _____. His response is not what matters.

2. If you have unresolved issues with mom, you must create a strategy for making a clean break from mom and for creating a new normal in how you relate to her.

    *   You need to identify the specific issues that you're dealing with.

    *   You need to create and enforce healthy _____.

IV. GUIDELINES FOR DADS

1. If you're a dad, then it's never too _____ to close the gap with your son.

- You can't change the past, but you can make changes right now in how you relate to your son.

- Perhaps your son still needs to hear from you the three "essentials:"

  - I love you
  - I'm proud of you
  - You're good at something

2. Wounding your son to some degree is _____.

DISCUSSION / REFLECTION QUESTIONS

1. Have you released/forgiven your dad and assumed responsibility for your own life? If you could sit down and "bare your soul" to your father, what would you say to him?

2. Do you need to have a respectful but direct conversation with your dad? Do you need to establish some boundaries with mom? Discuss.

3. If you're a dad, what do your children need from you right now? Are there things you are doing (or not doing) that may cause them to be wounded later in life?

the RED ZONE WOUNDED

Man who hasn't healed:

Like a physical wound, an untreated emotional wound can infect everything around it. The resulting sickness can cause significant harm to the entire organism, be it a person, a marriage, a family or community. Here then, we take a look at the differences between a man who has experienced healing and a man who remains wounded.

- Unable to fully live in the present, because part of his soul remains rooted in his past.

- Easily angered. His anger spills over onto others who aren't the real cause or source of his wounds.

- May have difficulty extending genuine forgiveness to others in spite of a sincere desire to do so.

- Questions his self-worth, lacks confidence, blames himself for conflicts or failures that may have had little or nothing to do with him.

- May struggle to trust or experience intimacy with spouse or those who could be close friends. May subconsciously sabotage relationships to minimize the risk of being wounded by someone else.

- Incapable of living the life of Authentic Manhood God made him to live because his wounds continue to fester, perhaps even growing and wounding others.

Man who has healed:

- At peace with his past, able to fully live in the present and move boldly into his future.

- Anger no longer bubbling just beneath the surface; instead his wrath is typically reserved for people and situations that merit righteous anger.

- Capable of exercising real, complete forgiveness and experiencing the benefits of a soul free of maintaining a list of ways he's been wronged.

- Finds his self-worth in his position as an adopted son of God, created, rescued and valued by a Father who will never fail or disown him.

- Capable of intimacy with his spouse and close friends. Willing to take the risk of being vulnerable with others and making himself fully known.

- Able to recognize and love God as "Father." Willing to cede control of his life to One he knows can be fully trusted.

- Capable of living the life of Authentic Manhood God made him to live. Equipped to help others find healing for the wounds in their soul.

SUPPORTING RESOURCES

Allender, Dan B. *The Healing Path: How the Hurts of Your Past Can Lead You to A More Abundant Life*. Waterbrook Press, 2000. Psycologist and author Dan Allender lays out guidelines on how to heal from the pain we've experienced in life.

Cloud, Henry and John Townsend. *Boundaries: When to Say Yes, When to Say No, To Take Control of Your Life*. Zondervan , 1992. Christian psychologists Henry Cloud and John Townsend offer insight on how to create healthy "boundaries" in our interpersonal relationships.

All-Alone

SESSION **FIVE** | Training Guide

THIS SERIES CAN ALSO BE EXPERIENCED IN THE **33** APP

BILL SMITH – A DUCK HUNTING

DISCIPLER

A GREAT MODEL FOR MENTORING MEN

BY BRIAN GOINS[*]

[*]Brian Goines is the author of *Playing Hurt: A Guy's Strategy for a Winning Marriage.* playinghurt.org

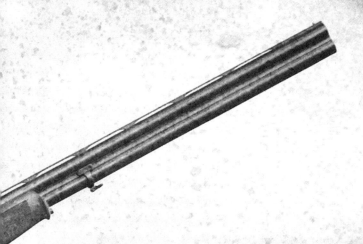

" **I**f Jesus of Nazareth had not been a Master Fisherman, the work of extending His kingdom among men would have ended with his death. If we do not learn and practice His art of fishing, or 'taking men alive,' we shall be failures in the chief work of His Kingdom on earth...every man is going to be 'taken alive' by someone. The Greek *zogreo*, meaning 'to take alive,' occurs only twice in the entire New Testament: in Luke 5:10 and 2 Timothy 2:26. In the one case, Jesus promises to enable His disciple to take men alive for the Kingdom. In the other case, Paul speaks of those who have been taken alive by the devil. By one or the other fisher of men every soul will eventually be taken..."

Excerpt from *Taking Men Alive*, Chapter 1 A formerly out of print book until Bill Smith read it, and now you can buy it on Amazon. Thanks Bill!

When Doug heard Robert Lewis' words he was pushing 40 with a successful construction materials company. He remembered his old mentors. He called them "coach." These men taught him how to tackle at the legs, snap the wrist when he shot the basketball, and hook his six-iron on purpose. But after graduation those mentors faded from view.

After 20 years of chasing success, Doug realized he wanted significance. He needed a new coach. He thought about talking to a pastor, but opted for a duck hunter.

Doug and his buddy, Gene, made an appointment with the first person that came to mind, Bill Smith. In another life Bill had flirted with ministry. After college, he had dabbled in seminary, but early on decided to chase earthly treasure rather than Christ. He spent a decade gaining the whole world through investments and in the process, he lost his soul and his marriage. Bill turned back to God and as one protégé remembered, "(He) threw himself into following God with the same stubborn, passionate fervor that he had given to pursuing the lies of the world."

"IF YOU DON'T HAVE A MENTOR, FIND ONE!"

By age 50, Bill had three main passions: God, his family (his second wife Cydney, an adopted daughter, and his two sons from his previous marriage), and ducks. He hunted all three fervently. People in the community knew Bill as a savvy investor and the original host for Men's Fraternity. Doug knew Bill as his couples' small group leader during the week, and duck stalker on the weekends.

Doug and Gene walked into Bill's office and sat around the small conference table. "So," Doug felt like he was back in 7th grade asking a girl to the dance, "Would you do what Robert talked about with us?" Bill thought about it. These two young men weren't looking for tips on how to pad their portfolios or master their "lonesome hen" duck call. "Sure," Bill retorted, "But you need to know boys, I don't have a job description for this mentoring stuff." So he created his own.

a couple of hours; then they gathered once a month; and finally they got together once a quarter. After graduating from their time with Bill they'd return to his office every now and again like former players coming back to see the old ball coach.

MENTORS MODEL A PASSION FOR GOD'S WORD

Bill kept the meetings simple, purpose-filled, and focused on the goal of making disciples. Doug remembered how each meeting required high priority (unless you lost a limb, you kept the appointment), high transparency (with Bill airing his laundry first), and a high regard for Scripture. They opened up the Bible and Bill peppered the air with questions. Guys later realized he knew most all of the answers, but he loved seeing men discover it for themselves.

Bill coached beyond the conference table. Whenever he would go speak, Bill always took a guy or two with him. Rather than hog the platform Bill gave his young guns the chance to share their story. Doug remembers Bill saying, "Doug, always be ready to share your story in three minutes or 23 minutes."

Unlike many men's small groups, Bill didn't believe in meeting for meeting's sake. Like a sport fisherman, he caught and released guys. At first, he met with men twice a month for

MENTORS BELIEVE INDIVIDUAL WORK IS THE GREATEST WORK

Like many believers, Bill loved the church. Early in his new journey, he tithed regularly, read his Bible, led small groups, but by-in-large he outsourced the Great Commission to the church pastors. Then he stumbled across Dr. Trumball. A business friend sent Bill a copy of a book originally published in 1905 but long since out of print. It detailed the principles of "man-winning" described by a Civil War chaplain, Dr. Henry Clay Trumball. On page one, Bill read **"the individual work of soul-winning is the greatest work that God permits men to do...it is the hardest work in the world to do..."**

A spark alighted in Bill's heart. He moved from investing with money to investing in men. Dr. Trumball wrote, "You cannot reach a thousand unless you reach one. The greatest preaching in the world is the preaching to an individual." Too many of us believe God only works through celebrity pastors who impact thousands at a conference. Yet every day God chooses to impact individuals around a conference table through duck hunting investors like Bill Smith. **After all, Jesus abandoned the crowds for a dozen men. He changed the world by changing a few.**

MENTORS REMIND YOUNG MEN OF THEIR MORTALITY

Our legacies won't change on their own. It requires bold, risky, and sacrificial moves. When Doug and Gene walked into Bill's office, Bill never imagined his lifespan was nearly complete. If Bill's life could be compared to a week, he was on Friday with Saturday coming quickly. Fortunately, years before the doctors had diagnosed him with prostate cancer, God used Doug and Gene's question, "Will you mentor us?" to launch Bill down a 10-year path of "taking men alive."

Shortly before Bill's death, Robert Lewis asked him to share his story at a Men's Fraternity session that was part of the series titled, *The Great Adventure*. Bill gave six observations from a terminally ill patient. Those seven minutes of video are well worth interrupting your day and can be viewed online at **authenticmanhood.com**.

In his message, Bill shared from Psalm 139:16, "Your eyes have seen my unformed substance; and in Your book were all written the days that were ordained for me, when as yet there was not one of them." Bill took time seriously because you never know when the clock runs out. The writer of Proverbs states, "He who pursues worthless things lacks sense" (12:11).

We all die. Whether we are 18 or 81, only God knows how much time we have left. We will spend those days hunting something either worthless or worthwhile. In his last 10 years Bill began living with a single-minded focus: to see young men take hold of their destiny.

WHAT TYPE OF MAN DO YOU WANT TO BE?

At Bill's funeral no one dropped a rose on his coffin and said, "Thanks for enlarging my portfolio." During the service, seats were filled with men whom Bill had poured into during the last decade of his life.

Men like John, who was a college kid when Bill invited him to the duck club: "I was 18 and in my first year of college when he took me, my good friend, and his dad hunting. Bill had white hair and a deep voice. After dinner, we sat around and blew our duck calls and I was proud to show off my duck-calling chops. Then Bill shared his story with us. He talked about the wealth and fame he had acquired and abused, how he had everything and nothing. Bill cried out to God for help and dedicated his life to follow Christ. Then, out of nowhere, Bill stared at me with those falcon-eyes and asked, 'John, what kind of man do you want to be?' I wasn't sure how to answer, so I mumbled something to which Bill replied, 'Well, that's a good start. I would love to help you with that.' And for the next 10 years, Bill did just that." John now spends his time leading a mentoring effort among the fatherless (**fatherlessgeneration.com**). 33

"IF YOU DON'T HAVE A MENTOR, FIND ONE!"

1. Identify someone you respect and ask them.

2. Set realistic expectations. They may say no for a variety of reasons that have nothing to do with you.

3. Remember, he is a mentor, not your dad. Don't expect him to fill that void in your life.

4. Develop a plan for your meetings: How often? How will they be structured?

5. Do some activity together: hunting, fishing, camping, or golfing.

Join the conversation about this article

facebook facebook.com/33theseries
twitter @33theseries

33 Presenter Insight

Getting Your Heart in the Game
by Bryan Carter, 33 Presenter

The heart is the most important spiritual part of your life. Solomon tells us this in Proverbs 4:23, "Above all else guard your heart for it is the wellspring of life." Our hearts are the center of our beings and serve as the core of the real you. Dallas Willard defines the heart as, "the executive center of a human life." The heart is our will, our emotions and our thoughts.

Most men grow up giving little value to their hearts. We were taught not to express our emotions, but to be strong regardless of the situation. We were told to "suck it up" and "be a man." Ultimately, this produced men who are consumed with living out of their minds with a rational and logical approach to life. When we add to that our personal heart wounds, from those who have hurt us by what they said or did to us, it's easy to begin to distance ourselves from that pain and others. We become the typical distant, unemotional and friendless man. Many times we may have "friends" but lack true depth in these friendships.

"We don't build relationships with our head, we build relationships with our heart."

Getting your heart in the game is the key to every man being able to overcome the "all-alone wound." The "all-alone wound" is a reflection of a distant and closed heart. The heart is the place where we connect with others. We don't build relationships with our head, we build relationships with our hearts. We build businesses with our heads, but we build a legacy with our hearts.

The heart is where we are able to have authentic conversations about life. The heart is where we can be honest about our struggles and failures. The heart is where we can discuss our fears and dreams. The heart is where we find accountability. *The heart has to be engaged to experience real connection. If my heart is not engaged, my relationships will remain shallow and superficial.*

The Bible celebrates the friendship of David and Jonathan as an amazing illustration of friendship between two men with open hearts. When men embrace their need for other godly men in their lives, they are both deeply enriched. There is no doubt we need friendships in our lives, yet quality friendships only happen as we connect at the heart level.

For most of my life I lived disconnected from my heart. *As I have grown as a man, my greatest joy has been getting my heart in the game.* 33

Strategies to get your heart in the game

- Embrace the value that your heart brings to life.

- Pray for God to send you teammates or to identify friendships to you that need to deepen.

- Spend quality time with your friends in order to build deeper relationships.

- Seek to have deeper conversations about life in addition to those surface conversations about sports, cars and hobbies.

- Learn to ask meaningful questions and share honestly about your dreams, fears and struggles.

Join the conversation about this article

facebook facebook.com/33theseries
twitter @33theseries

‖Cigar Shop Community

by Cliff Jordan

Even authentic men can have a problem coming together and forming tight friendships with one another. However, since the beginning of time, hunting and combat were two major forces that drew groups of men together and saw brotherhoods formed. Today we see similar experiences happening in hunting fields and on football fields everywhere. Men who have been through a battle together—whether in real combat or on the gridiron—often times say that they form different bonds than they do with men whom they meet at other times in life. Something about those experiences changes things. Is it the violence? The danger? The fighting for a common goal? I can't really describe what it is, but I know what it isn't...phony. Authentic Men can't stand phony, contrived experiences.

When was the last time you gathered with other men for a book club? A painting party? The very thought of attending one of those groups would make most men break out in hives. If you're not on the battlefield or football field with a group of guys, then where are the opportunities for men to gather in masculine ways that seem natural for them? What is the church doing, if anything, to provide opportunities for men to connect?

We are in a battle for manhood, and men need environments to rally around each other, to fight for one another and for a common cause. A guy named Bob Miller looked outside the four walls of the church building to create an environment where this coming together could take place. This is the story of how Miller embraced the community

platform offered by many men's love of fine cigars to promote and foster an environment of Authentic Manhood.

City Cigars is a cigar shop owned by Miller, a man who is passionate about connecting men to each other and to their Creator. *The cigar shop was started, in part, to be that environment that facilitated an atmosphere where men could get together in a non-threatening environment.* What Miller found was that when men exhaled the smoke out from a cigar, much more came out than just smoke. The cares and burdens of the day came out as well. This lowered men's guards and prepared them to be authentic with each other.

A small group of men, who were regulars at the shop, began meeting and discussing Authentic Manhood together. Through that experience, the men began talking with men outside the group about the challenges of manhood, and that small group grew. It's now a thriving group of courageous men who are facing the challenges of manhood in community with each other. Does it have to be a cigar shop? No. Do men need environments where they can be authentic with each other? Yes. *Look for places where men naturally congregate and where they are naturally encouraged to be authentic.* Next, facilitate a community of committed men to make progress in the journey God has created them for. If that place can't be found, it's always an opportunity to unleash your entrepreneurial spirit and create something! 33

Join the conversation about this article

facebook   facebook.com/33theseries
twitter   @33theseries

All-Alone Presented by Bryan Carter

I. INTRODUCTION

1. Today, we are going to talk about the _____ of a man's relationship with other men and how those relationships or lack of them can affect a man.

2. We are also going to introduce you to a different type of wound, a wound that is self-inflicted, called, the All-Alone wound.

3. This wound characterizes a man who attempts to live life alone.

4. _____ in life are essential for us to become better men.

II. THREE TYPES OF TEAMMATES THAT BLESS AND ENERGIZE A MAN'S LIFE

1. The Encouraging _____

    •   Having someone in your life who is a step ahead of you and can offer you wisdom and guidance.

    •   It's someone who takes a special interest in you.

    •   They are committed to your development.

    •   They see the _____ in you even when you can't see it in yourself.

    •   They are someone you admire and respect.

2. The _____ Teammate

    •   Blessed is the man who has a few committed teammates.

    •   They love you unconditionally but will speak truth into your life.

    •   They are true friends who are committed to your best.

    •   Professor Geoffery Greif says: "Some men remain _____ in the adolescent phase of friendship."

- You must take the risk of creating these side-by-side friendships.

3. The Eager _____

   - Someone who is a step behind you in life but eager to learn from your experiences.

   - You have the opportunity to give back and _____ in others.

III. THE ALL-ALONE WOUND

1. Comes from the tendency of a man to live life _____ of character shaping relationships.

2. This self-inflicted wound is _____.

3. The all-alone wound is a social, emotional and spiritual loss caused by the lack of healthy male teammates.

4. Most men are never truly _____.

IV. THE CONSEQUENCES OF THE ALL-ALONE WOUND

1. A warped perspective on life

   • Self-deceit comes from being disconnected.

   • "There is a way that seems right to a man, but its end is the way to death."
     Proverbs 14:12 (ESV)

   • To get an accurate picture of yourself, you need feedback from trusted teammates.

2. The potential for careless living and _____ choices.

   • "Whoever isolates himself seeks his own desire; he breaks out against sound
     judgement." Proverbs 18:1 (ESV)

   • Not having a teammate makes it easy for the _____
     to get lowered.

   • The path to foolish decisions is often aloneness.

3.   A lost chance for much needed transparency

   •   Every man needs teammates with whom he can feel _____.

   •   Without transparency, men are likely to fall into:

      ○   Discouragement
      ○   Depression
      ○   Danger

v. BUILDING HEALTHY TEAMMATES

1.   Learn how to be a _____ teammate who encourages others.

2.   Learn how to ask good questions and take a genuine _____ in others.

3.   Be willing to be vulnerable and _____.

4. _____ with other men.

VI. INITIATING WITH MENTORS AND PROTÉGÉS

"Whoever walks with the wise becomes wise, but the companion of fools will suffer harm."
Proverbs 13:20 (ESV)

1. Mentors

   • Look for a man whose character and skills you _____.

   • Consider having different mentors for different areas of life.

   • Consider having mentors from different _____ of life.

2. Protégé

   • Be a man to whom others are _____

   • Make yourself available.

   • "Two are better than one, because they have a good reward for their toil."
     Ecclesiastes 4:9 (NIV)

DISCUSSION / REFLECTION QUESTIONS

1.   Do you feel the all-alone wound? Explain.

2.   Discuss your level of true transparency with other men in your life.

3.   What are the next steps you need to take to initiate with teammates in your life?

the RED ZONE

ISOLATION

"Most men lead lives of quiet desperation and go to the grave with the song still in them."

Henry David Thoreau

An ever-increasing number of studies show that men are living lives of isolation. While technology allows us to be more connected than ever, statistics prove that the quality and depth of those connections is sorely lacking.

- About **one-third of men** state that they "often feel very lonely."

- From **1940** to **2000**, the number of **single person households increased** from **7** percent to almost **25** percent.

- About **one-quarter of fathers with children** state that they "often feel very lonely."

- **Many men rely solely on their wives or partners for social and emotional needs.** Women generally have a broader social network to draw upon to meet their needs.

- **Men rely more on employers and co-workers as a source to provide personal support** than with friendships out of the office.

- In the most recent **19-year period**, the number of people who said there was **no one with whom they could discuss important matters tripled**.

- **Men without a single confidant** made up nearly **one-quarter** of those surveyed.

- **One** man in **ten** has a friend with whom he discusses work, money, marriage; only **one** in more than **twenty** has a friendship where he discloses his feelings about himself.

Sources: counsellingconnection.com; General Social Survey, Duke University, Miller McPherson; The McGill Report on Male Intimacy, Michael McGill; Buddy System: Understanding Male Friendships, Geoffrey Greif; United States Census, 2000; Capitalism and Loneliness: Why Pornography Is a Multibillion-Dollar Industry, Tess Fraad Wolff and Harriet Fraad, Truthout; American Foundation for Suicide Prevention

SCRIPTURE REFERENCES

Proverbs 14:12 (ESV) "There is a way that seems right to a man, but its end is the way to death."

Proverbs 18:1 (ESV) "Whoever isolates himself seeks his own desire; he breaks out against all sound judgment."

Proverbs 13:20 (ESV) "Whoever walks with the wise becomes wise, but the companion of fools will suffer harm."

Ecclesiastes 4:9 (NIV) "Two are better than one, because they have a good reward for their toil."

SUPPORTING RESOURCES

Weber, Stu. *Locking Arms: God's Design for Masculine Friendships.* Multnomah, 1995.

Heart

SESSION **SIX** | Training Guide

THIS SERIES CAN ALSO BE EXPERIENCED IN THE **33** APP

The tumbleweed has become a common symbol for desolation.

DON'T be a SPIRITUAL TUMBLEWEED

by Jeff Lawrence

The first time I saw a tumbleweed, I was riding in the back of a legal-pad-yellow station wagon on the way to Colorado. We were on a family vacation, and Dad was doing his best Chevy Chase impersonation. The highway stretched out ahead of us as far as the horizon. No hills and no turns. This was a road you could fall asleep on and wake up later to find nothing had changed. The rare tinge of excitement came when a tumbleweed would blow across the road.

You may never have seen a tumbleweed, but the name itself gives you a decent idea what one looks like. A tumbleweed is a small bundle of air and twigs, bouncing around like a beach ball on a windy day, but without the color and fun. If you've ever seen a Western film, you've probably watched one roll across the arid terrain just before a shootout. It is a lifeless, leafless, colorless, weightless weed that tumbles around the world without a purpose. The real issue for the tumbleweed, however, is not what you see but what you do not see. Tumbleweeds have no root system. Nothing nourishes them against the parched land, and nothing anchors them in the ground so that they can withstand gusts of wind. **The problem is not what exists above ground, the real trouble lies beneath the surface.[1] Men are like that too.**

1 R. Kent Hughes, Colossians and Philemon: The Supremacy of Christ in Preaching the Word Series. (Crossway Books,1989) chapter 7, p. 62.

2 These ideas have been influenced by pastor and author Timothy J. Keller, Paul's Letter to the Galatians, Leaders Guide (Redeemer Presbyterian Church, 2003).

The Bible says some people are tossed every which way by the winds. They are spiritual tumbleweeds. When the wind blows through their lives, they are untethered and tossed around. When the storms come, they lose their bearings. When temptation comes, they are led astray. When false teachings cross the airwaves, they are confused. When life doesn't go as planned, they are sent reeling.

The Bible also describes another way to live. It tells of men that are strong, steadfast, immovable. They are tenacious in times of trial and joyful even in hardship. They hold their ground when life knocks them around. We need more of these men. God didn't design you to be tossed around by every wind that blows through your life. You were created for deep connection to Jesus that anchors you and causes you to flourish. But it's not what happens on the surface that makes you strong. **It's what happens inside that makes all the difference.**

Psalm 63 says, "O God, you are my God; earnestly I will seek you; my soul thirsts for you; my flesh yearns for you, as in a dry and weary land where there is not water."

These verses have long been some of my favorite in all the Bible. When life is beating me up, these verses point me to the source of strength and sustenance. God alone is sufficient for that task. The writer of this psalm says, "You are my God." You are not my buddy or therapist or team captain or head of my religion. You are my God. You are the Sovereign King of the Universe, but in your mercy and grace and love for me, you are also mine. Earnestly is not a word we use very often, but you might think of it as pursuing something passionately, doggedly, and with great determination.

When we seek something in that manner, it is because we believe that it is of great value. We do so because our well-being and our joy are dependent upon our connection to God. I talk to many men who say, "I want that kind of connection with God." And then they add, "But how?" This is the point at which we are going to have to do some serious work. The wrong approach will exhaust you without ever addressing the core issue.

Many guys focus on the external part of life and avoid the internal realm of the heart. They try to up their activity level to solve their problems. So, they work harder at reading their Bibles, limiting their drinking, controlling their tempers, or spending more time with their families. All of these are good things, even necessary things, but they are not the primary thing.

We learn much about seeking God in Colossians 2:6-7 (ESV), "Therefore, as you received Christ Jesus the Lord, so walk **in him**, rooted and built up **in him** and established in the faith, just as you were taught, abounding in thanksgiving."

I believe the core idea of the spiritual life is found in these two verses: life is found in him; not in me. In a single sentence, the phrase "in him" shows up or is implied five times. We receive him, walk in him, are rooted in him, are built up in him, and are established by faith in him.

We receive him, walk in him, are rooted in him, are built up in him, and are established by faith in him.

Do you get the sense that Jesus is kind of a big deal? It is all about Jesus. When you dig into these verses, you see how everything in our spiritual pursuit is tied to Him. You receive Jesus through no merit of your own but as a free gift of grace that you received through faith. You were a sinner, but in him you have been called righteous. You were headed for eternal death, but in him you have eternal life. You were in darkness, but in him you were transferred to the kingdom of light. You were in exile, but in him you've been made a friend. You were an outsider, but in him you have been invited to the party.

Gospel-roots provide
nourishment & strength

You were an enemy, but in him you have been made an adopted son of the King.

Some of you have been hurt by a religiosity that tried to clean up the externals of your life to the neglect of your heart. They tried to fix your morality or your appearance or your way of thinking, but it had no power to change your heart. What gives you new life is not your deeds or discipline or determination or doctrinal adherence but your Savior.

The gospel, or good news, of Jesus says that, though the wounds and scars and brokenness of your heart run deeper than you ever realized, the grace of Jesus is bigger and stronger than you ever imagined.[2] No matter what darkness you find when you do an honest exploration of your heart, Jesus is neither surprised nor worried about what is there. He can handle all your sin. In him, you can live with joy no matter what fault lines run through your heart.

If we want to avoid the spiritual tumbleweed syndrome, we will deeply root our lives in the gospel of Jesus. As healthy Christ-followers, we develop a gospel root system in our hearts so extensive that nothing can shake us. We grow roots of prayerfulness so that we enjoy friendship with Jesus more and more. We grow roots in service so that we have a genuine love for people that Jesus loves. We grow roots of obedience so that our desires no longer burn for things that cannot truly satisfy us. We grow roots of worship so that our heart's affections yearn more strongly for Jesus.

Gospel-roots provide nourishment and strength so that we are built up to maturity and are established in the faith. This kind of life transformation does not occur because of what is in me, it happens because I am walking with him, living in him, trusting in him, obeying in him, secure in him. This gives us both confidence and humility.

As long as you are depending on yourself, you are a slave to the wounds and scars and brokenness of your heart. But when you have life in Him, healing and freedom and wholeness are possible. You are as strong as the life source to which you are connected, and Jesus is infinitely strong.

God did not plan to fill the world with spiritual tumbleweeds. Jesus said, "I came that they may have life and have it abundantly" (John 10:10 ESV). He intended for his people to thrive and grow. For the sake of our friends and families, our churches, our communities, and our world, may we increasingly be gospel-rooted men whose lives are marked by strength and fruitfulness and purpose. 33

Join the conversation about this article

facebook facebook.com/33theseries
twitter @33theseries

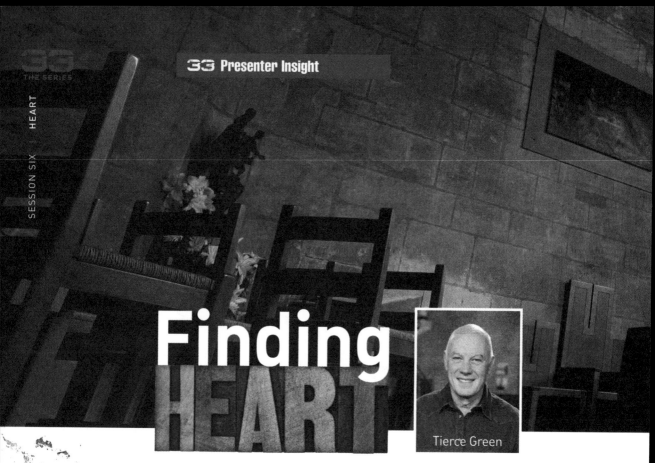

Finding HEART

Tierce Green

by James Pecht

Tierce Green had to get out of church to find God.

At the age of 10, after the death of his father, his mother made sure he attended church. She had hoped it would instill values and a sense of direction. She hoped it would melt his heart. Instead, Tierce says, church became a place of rules and regulations – and little else.

"When I graduated from high school, I thought I'd been there and done that. I didn't want to do this again," he said. So when he went off to college, he left the church behind.

"I was pretty smart; I went to college on an academic scholarship, and I thought that I could guess and find meaning on my own," he says. "But I really couldn't."

Tierce says he needed a community with heart to help him find his own heart. And he found that community the summer after his freshman year in college. They weren't overzealous and they weren't what he calls "churchy." They were authentic and caring, and they lived from their hearts.

"They showed me what God was really like," Tierce says. "In them, I saw authenticity. I saw a relational experience with God. And that's what finally made church come alive."

Tierce says too many people confuse the word "religion" with "relationship." Instead of truly inviting God into their lives and holding an ongoing conversation with Him, they find it easier to keep everything at arm's length. They'll

get caught up in following the rules and being "perfect" Christians, and they miss out on what God really wants from us.

"You clock in; you clock out. You do your time and you feel like you're good."

So what exactly does God want from us? Tierce says it's clearly spelled out in scripture: "To act justly and to love mercy and to walk humbly with your God." (Micah 6:8)

"God wants us to humble ourselves and realize that we don't have it all figured out," Tierce says. "We need Him, and we need to love Him and to love others."

And that means opening up your heart to receive God into your life.

A church environment can serve as a powerful tool to love and support others, and to help you open your heart. But it's not the only place that can help.

"We know we need that interaction with other people because we're not designed to go through life solo. Church is important for that interaction with others. There's accountability and the support we need. But a lot of people will substitute church for that relationship with God," and that's where they lose their way.

"Church can be a good thing. But church without meaning and without a relationship with God is a colossal waste of time. It's just empty and frustrating." In other words, it lacks heart. 33

Join the conversation about this article

facebook facebook.com/33theseries

twitter @33theseries

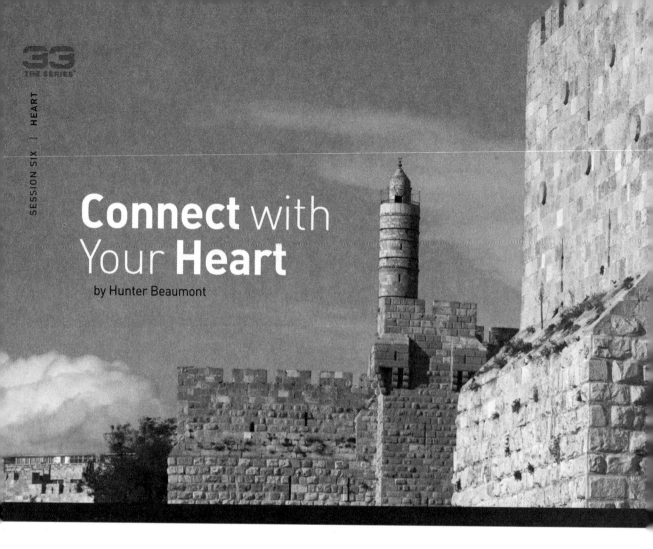

Connect with Your Heart

by Hunter Beaumont

A man who heeds an upward call – rejecting passivity, accepting responsibility, leading courageously, investing eternally – is signing up for a spiritual fight. He's sure to be confronted with the usual emotions of battle: confusion, discouragement, fatigue, fear and anger.

And herein lies a challenge. We need to be able to express these emotions to God. But how? "Staying connected to your heart" and "communicating at an emotional level" is not typical boot camp training. *Fortunately, God inspired an entire book to help men connect with their heart, and it's the easiest one to find.* Open any Bible to the middle, and there you meet the Psalms.

Years ago, a friend introduced me to praying through the Psalms. For a man who sometimes stammers and mumbles when asked, "How are you feeling," I surprisingly found a voice. As if God knew I needed help, he inspired a book of mentors.

Feeling overwhelmed? Open to *Psalm 5*: "Give ear to my words, O Lord; consider my groaning. Give attention to the sound of my cry." Anxious? I turn the page to *Psalm 6*: "My soul also is greatly troubled. But you, O Lord – how long?" When frustration sets in, I flee to *Psalm 16*: "I bless the Lord who gives me counsel; in the night also my heart instructs me. I have set the Lord always before me; because He is at my right hand, I shall not be shaken."

The emotions of these Psalms are so naked, so unbridled that I sometimes blush. "Can I say that to God?" On this question, author Patrick Henry Reardon has been helpful. He counsels, "To relinquish any one of the psalms on the excuse that its sentiments are too violent for a Christian is a clear sign that a person has also given up the very battle that a Christian is summoned from his bed to fight. *The psalms are prayers for those engaged in an ongoing spiritual conflict. No one else need bother even opening the book.*" (*Christ in the Psalms*, 6).

Jesus evidently opened this book quite often. Drive nails through His hands and He bleeds out psalms. His final, anguished cry was clipped from *Psalm 22*: "My God! My

God! Why have you forsaken me?" Having said that, He breathed his last and finished well. 33

Join the conversation about this article

facebook facebook.com/33theseries

twitter @33theseries

SESSION SIX | HEART

Heart Presented by Tierce Green

I. INTRODUCTION

Wound: Any unresolved issue where a lack of closure adversely impacts and shapes the direction and dynamics of a man's life now.

1. All men are affected by _____ to one degree or another.

2. Authentic men are _____.

3. Every man has the _____ wound.

II. A BROKEN WORLD

1. In an instant, a perfect world became _____.

2. We live as broken men in a broken world.

3. In spite of our best efforts to create_____ on earth, we still experience pain, disappointment, discouragement, fear, anxiety, and frustration.

4. One day Jesus will return to make all things _____.

    *   "He will wipe away every tear from their eyes, and death shall be no more, neither shall there be mourning, nor crying, nor pain anymore, for the former things have passed away." Revelation 21:4 (ESV)

III. BROKEN MEN

1. Adam's sin not only broke the world, it also broke _____.

2. The Bible teaches that our nature is bent _____ from God.

3. Left to ourselves we try to do _____ but too often we can't.

4. The heart wound is a man's total inability to do good before God apart from a relationship with Jesus Christ.

    • "There is no one righteous, not even one." Romans 3:10 (NIV)

    • Compared to God's standard, we all fall miserably _____.

5. The solution to the heart wound is not psychology, morality, religion, or self-help.

6. In the book of Romans, Paul reveals the _____ to the heart wound:

    • "While we were still sinners, Christ died for us." Romans 5:8 (ESV)

    • Jesus said, "I am the way, the truth, and the life. No one comes to the Father except through me." John 14:6 (ESV)

7. Jesus is our only solution to the heart wound

IV. DISCONNECTED MEN

1. Faith in Jesus doesn't mean that we all of a sudden become _____.

2. There are _____ effects of the heart wound.

3. When we disconnect from our _____ it sets us up for failure and it leads us into dangerous and damaging territory.

4. Men have a tendency to bore through life with their _____.

5. Men's routine _____ of self-disclosure is dangerous to their emotional and even physical health.

6. Author Chip Dodd says: "We just go through the motions, never fully knowing ourselves, never fully knowing others and never fully finding the _____ life."

7. Those feelings and experiences that we stuff deep inside always find a way to the _____.

v. THREE SUGGESTIONS FOR CONNECTING WITH OUR HEART

1. We must recognize and _____ feelings.

    - "Feeling our feelings is about beginning to take responsibility for the content of our hearts. It requires us to live out of how our hearts are made and use our feelings to experience and add to relationship, first with ourselves, then with others."

    - There are two extremes that can happen with emotions:

        - To _____ - driven by desire to control life.

        - To _____ emotions - driven by self-love and self-obsession.

    - A balanced approach is to be honest with our feelings before God and before trustworthy friends.

2. We must tell the _____ about our hearts to those who are trustworthy.

    - We need to practice _____ communication.

    - To one degree or another, we all struggle with the _____ things.

    - "No temptation has seized you except what is common to man." 1 Corinthians 10:13 (NIV)

3. Give the truth of your heart to _____.

    - Like David, we must be brutally _____ with God.

    - Try keeping a journal of your prayers to God

VI. CONCLUSION

1. To stay connected to our heart, we need three things:

    *   Feel our feelings
    *   Tell the truth about our hearts to others
    *   Give the truth of our heart to God

2. We are _____ men living in a broken world.

    • Jesus said, "I have told you these things, so that in me you may have peace. In the world you will have trouble. But take heart! I have overcome the world." John 16:33 (NIV)

3. We are wired to have _____ with our Creator and community with others.

4. The six sessions of "A Man and His Story" were intended to help you become more connected:

    *   Connected to your past...with your wounds and your victories (sessions 1, 2, 3 & 4).
    *   Connected to others...your teammates (session 5).
    *   Connected to yourself...your own heart (session 6).
    *   Connected to God...and the story He is telling through your life (sessions 1 and 6).

DISCUSSION/ REFLECTION QUESTIONS

1. How has the brokenness of the world touched your life? What does God's promise to redeem the world mean to you?

2. Why do you think it is difficult for guys to be transparent? Discuss how transparency may be difficult for you personally.

3. This session recommended three ways to connect with your heart. How are you doing in these areas:

    1. Recognize and feel feelings
    2. Tell the truth about our hearts to those who are trustworthy
    3. Give the truth of our heart to God

Facing the heart wound without Jesus Christ is impossible. To view a Gospel presentation that can help you or someone you know, visit **authenticmanhood.com**.

unashamed

I am not ashamed of the gospel, because it is the power of God for the salvation of everyone who believes; first for the Jew, then for the Gentile. For in the gospel a righteousness from God is revealed, a righteousness that is by faith from first to last, just as it is written: "The righteous will live by faith."

Paul the Apostle, Romans 1:16-17

Fellowship of the Unashamed Dr. Bob Moorehead

I am a part of the fellowship of the Unashamed. I have the Holy Spirit Power. The die has been cast. I have stepped over the line. The decision has been made. I am a disciple of Jesus Christ. I won't look back, let up, slow down, back away, or be still. My past is redeemed, my present makes sense, and my future is secure. I am finished and done with low living, sight walking, small planning, smooth knees, colorless dreams, tame visions, mundane talking, chintzy giving, and dwarfed goals.

I no longer need preeminence, prosperity, position, promotions, plaudits, or popularity. I don't have to be right, first, tops, recognized, praised, regarded, or rewarded. I now live by presence, learn by faith, love by patience, live by prayer, and labor by power.

My pace is set, my gait is fast, my goal is Heaven, my road is narrow, my way is rough, my companions few, my Guide is reliable, my mission is clear. I cannot be bought, compromised, deterred, lured away, turned back, diluted, or delayed. I will not flinch in the face of sacrifice, hesitate in the presence of adversity, negotiate at the table of the enemy, ponder at the pool of popularity, or meander in the maze of mediocrity.

I won't give up, back up, let up, or shut up until I've preached up, prayed up, paid up, stored up, and stayed up for the cause of Christ. I am a disciple of Jesus Christ. I must go until He returns, give until I drop, preach until all know, and work until He comes.

And when He comes to get His own, He will have no problem recognizing me. My colors will be clear for "I am not ashamed of the Gospel, because it is the power of God for the salvation of everyone who believes."

SCRIPTURE REFERENCES

Revelation 21:4 (ESV) "He will wipe away every tear from their eyes, and death shall be no more, neither shall there be mourning, nor crying, nor pain anymore, for the former things have passed away."

Romans 3:10-12 (NIV) "As it is written: 'There is no one righteous, not even one; there is no one who understands, no one who seeks God. All have turned away, they have together become worthless; there is no one who does good, not even one.'"

Romans 5:8 (ESV) "But God shows his love for us in that while we were still sinners, Christ died for us."

John 14:6 (ESV) "Jesus said to him, 'I am the way, and the truth, and the life. No one comes to the Father except through me.'"

1 Corinthians 10:13 (NIV) "No temptation has seized you except what is common to man. And God is faithful; he will not let you be tempted beyond what you can bear. But when you are tempted, he will also provide a way out so that you can stand up under it."

John 16:33 (NIV) "I have told you these things, so that in me you may have peace. In this world you will have trouble. But take heart! I have overcome the world."

SUPPORTING RESOURCES

Allender, Dan B. *Men to Boys: Leading with a Limp: Take Full Advantage of Your Most Powerful Weakness.* Waterbrook Press, 2006. Psychologist, Dan Allender, argues that flaws and brokenness can be valuable traits for leaders. We must move beyond trying to hide our weakness.

Dodd, Chip. *A Voice of the Heart: A Call to Full Living.* Nashville: Sage Hill Resources, 2001. In this book, counselor Chip Dodd provides guidance for understanding the experiences of the heart. Topics include hurt, loneliness, sadness, anger, fear, shame, guilt, and gladness.

ACTION PLAN

YOUR STRATEGIC MOVE | SESSION ONE : **LOOKING BACK**

_____

_____

YOUR STRATEGIC MOVE | SESSION TWO : **DAD**

_____

_____

YOUR STRATEGIC MOVE | SESSION THREE : **MOM**

_____

_____

YOUR STRATEGIC MOVE | SESSION FOUR : **HEALING**

_____

_____

YOUR STRATEGIC MOVE | SESSION FIVE : **ALL-ALONE**

_____

_____

YOUR STRATEGIC MOVE | SESSION SIX : **HEART**

_____

_____

A Man and His Story - Answer Key

SESSION ONE: LOOKING BACK

I. 1. Story
II. 2. Driven
    4. Sacred
III. 1. Balanced
    2. Wounds
        • Pretend
        • Unresolved
    3. Author

SESSION TWO: DAD

I. 1. Absent
    4. Admiration
    5. 33%
    6.
        • Uniquely
II. 2. Relationship
    4. Related
III. 1.
        • Anger
        • Vacuum
    2.
        • Pretend
        • Demands
    3.
        • Relational
        • Informational
IV. 2. Overcome
V. 1. Time
    3. Why
    4.
        • Lived

SESSION THREE: MOM

I. 1. Relationship
II. 1. Physical
    2. Emotional
        • Overly
        • Fragile
III. 1. Unhealthy
    2.
        • Controlling
        • Passive
IV. 2. Father
V. 1. Unintentional
    3. Release
    4. Gap
VI. 1. Conflict
    2.
        • Boundaries
    5.
        • Unfinished

SESSION FOUR: HEALING

II. 1. Responsibly
    2. Forgiveness
    3. Share
    4. Unresolved
III. 1. Direct
        • Response
    2.
        • Boundaries
IV. 1. Late
    2. Unavoidable

SESSION FIVE: ALL-ALONE

I. 1. Importance
    4. Teammates
II. 1. Mentor
      • Best
    2. Side-by-side
      • Stuck
    3. Protege
      • Invest
III. 1. Outside
    2. Avoidable
    4. Known
IV. 2. Foolish
      • Standard
    3.
      • Safe
V. 1. Loyal
    2. Interest
    3. Transparent
    4. Initiate
VI. 1.
      • Admire
      • Seasons
    2.
      • Drawn

SESSION SIX: HEART

I. 1. Wounds
    2. Difference-makers
    3. Heart
II. 1. Imperfect
    3. Heaven
    4. New
III. 1. Us
    2. Away
    3. Good
    4.
      • Short
    6. Solution
IV. 1. Perfect
    2. Lingering
    3. Heart
    4. Head
    5. Avoidance
    6. Abundant
    7. Surface
V. 1. Feel
      • Disconnect
      • Overindulge
    2. Truth
      • Transparent
      • Same
    3. God
      • Honest
VI. 2. Broken
    3. Community

authenticmanhood.com

- Other volumes of *33 The Series*
- ***Men's Fraternity Classic*** and *33 The Series* mobile apps
- Online video and audio downloads
- "Share Your Story" with others
- ***Men's Fraternity Classic*** curriculum